Brazilian History and Mythology

An Enthralling Journey Through Brazil's Past and Legendary Myths

© Copyright 2024 - All rights reserved.

The content contained within this book may not be reproduced, duplicated, or transmitted without direct written permission from the author or the publisher.

Under no circumstances will any blame or legal responsibility be held against the publisher, or author, for any damages, reparation, or monetary loss due to the information contained within this book, either directly or indirectly.

Legal Notice:

This book is copyright protected. It is only for personal use. You cannot amend, distribute, sell, use, quote, or paraphrase any part, or the content within this book, without the consent of the author or publisher.

Disclaimer Notice:

Please note the information contained within this document is for educational and entertainment purposes only. All effort has been executed to present accurate, up-to-date, reliable, and complete information. No warranties of any kind are declared or implied. Readers acknowledge that the author is not engaging in the rendering of legal, financial, medical, or professional advice. The content within this book has been derived from various sources. Please consult a licensed professional before attempting any techniques outlined in this book.

By reading this document, the reader agrees that under no circumstances is the author responsible for any losses, direct or indirect, that are incurred as a result of the use of the information contained within this document, including, but not limited to, errors, omissions, or inaccuracies.

Free limited time bonus

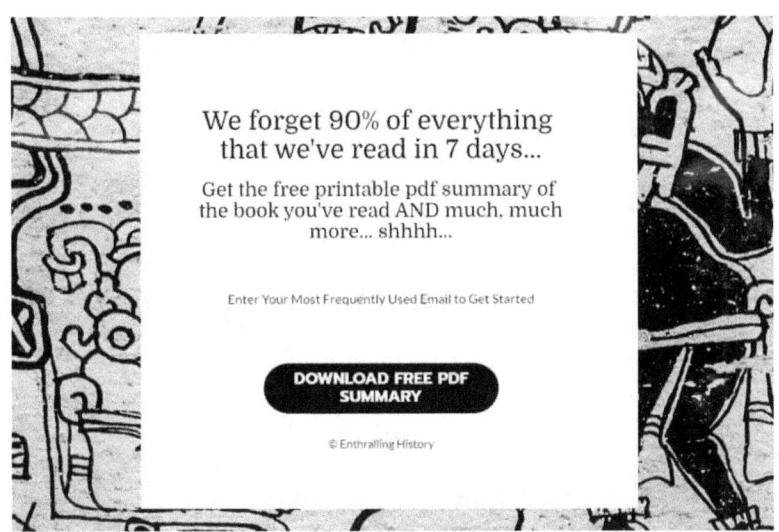

Stop for a moment. We have a free bonus set up for you. The problem is this: we forget 90% of everything that we read after 7 days. Crazy fact, right? Here's the solution: we've created a printable, 1-page pdf summary for this book that you're reading now. All you have to do to get your free pdf summary is to go to the following website:

https://livetolearn.lpages.co/enthrallinghistory/

Or, Scan the QR code!

Once you do, it will be intuitive. Enjoy, and thank you!

Table of Contents

PART 1: HISTORY OF BRAZIL 1
   INTRODUCTION 2
   CHAPTER ONE – THE ORIGINS OF COLONIAL BRAZIL 5
   CHAPTER TWO – PORTUGUESE BRAZIL 17
   CHAPTER THREE – THE BIRTH OF INDEPENDENT BRAZIL 31
   CHAPTER FOUR – FROM EMPIRE TO REPUBLIC 46
   CHAPTER FIVE – THE STRUGGLES OF THE BRAZILIAN
   REPUBLIC 63
   CHAPTER SIX – THE BIRTH OF MODERN BRAZIL 78
   CONCLUSION 90
PART 2: BRAZILIAN MYTHOLOGY 92
   INTRODUCTION 93
   CHAPTER ONE – THE CREATION MYTHS 97
   CHAPTER TWO – HIGH SPIRITS 109
   CHAPTER THREE – RIVER MYTHS 118
   CHAPTER FOUR – JAGUAR TALES 124
   CHAPTER FIVE – MONSTROUS BEASTS 131
   CHAPTER SIX – SERPENTS, SNAKES, AND WORMS 140
   CHAPTER SEVEN – BRAZILIAN BOGEYMEN 147
   CHAPTER EIGHT – AFRICAN INFLUENCES 153
   CHAPTER NINE – FOLKTALES AND FAIRYTALES 159
   CONCLUSION 165

HERE'S ANOTHER BOOK BY ENTHRALLING HISTORY THAT
YOU MIGHT LIKE... 169
FREE LIMITED TIME BONUS.. 170
SOURCES 171
IMAGE SOURCES 172

Part 1: History of Brazil

An Enthralling Guide to Ancient Indigenous Civilizations, Portuguese Colonization, the Imperial Era, and Modern Times

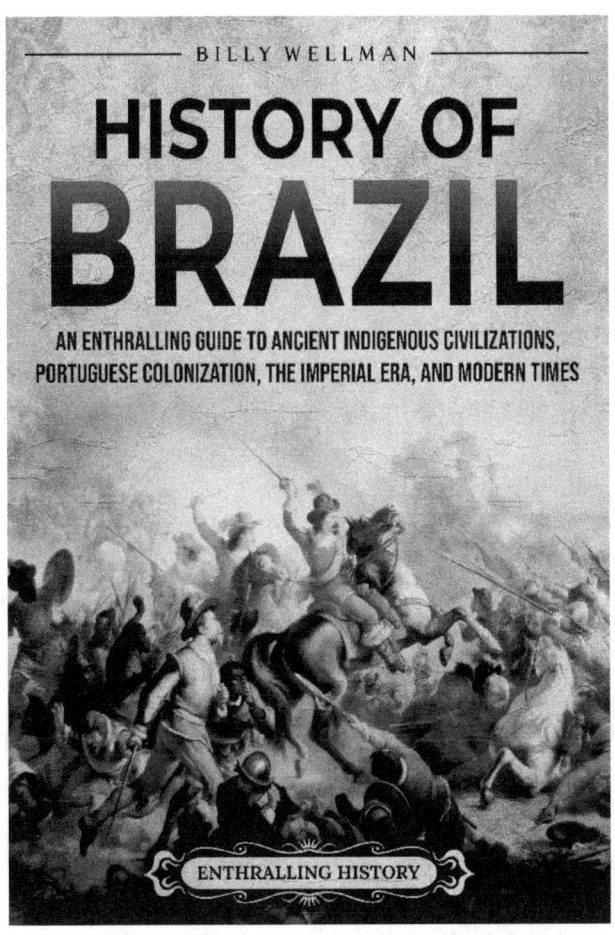

Introduction

Brazil boasts a uniquely vibrant culture, an eclectic mix of people from diverse social or ethnic backgrounds, and a rich and vast natural landscape. As one of the largest countries in the world and one of the most important politically, it is naturally very interesting to examine how it got there. How did Brazil become such a particularly remarkable country? Which developments led to one nation controlling such a huge chunk of land, full of surprises and secrets—some of which we are still unsure about? Who were some of the most important figures who shaped what Brazil is today?

The answers to these and many more questions about Brazil lie in the nation's history, which is very compelling to examine. It is a combination of dynamic and memorable events that capture the curiosity of people of all kinds, whether familiar with the broader context in which the history of Brazil must be placed or simply interested in finding out more about a country they love. Brazilian history certainly contains something for everyone and is full of occurrences that coincide with other social and historical circumstances around the world. This is true for both the pre- and post-Columbian eras, though we know far less about the former than about the latter.

The centuries-long struggle of the Brazilian people, which continues even today, is not just marked by their adverse relations with foreign conquerors and colonizers. One of the main struggles of the Brazilian people, including the Indigenous population and those who settled the nation after the arrival of Portuguese colonizers, was with European ideas.

Much like in other colonies in the Americas and around the world, efforts to Europeanize Brazil were prevalent. The colonizers brought a distinct set of ideas, attitudes, practices, and traditions, and their diffusion from Europe to Brazil accelerated during the eighteenth and nineteenth centuries.

European institutions and ways of thought were challenged by the Indigenous and African populations of Brazil, whose lives had been drastically affected by the age of European colonization. It can be argued that Brazil, the country as we know it today, was born only after these cultures synthesized with European culture. As we will see, they exerted their own influence on the colonizers, a process that culminated with the independence of Brazil in 1822—an event that transformed the socio-political landscape of the Western Hemisphere and affected the European power struggles in the "Old World."

Thus, it is interesting to closely examine Brazil's history and think about the most important developments that greatly influenced Brazil's evolution into its present form. A good way to do this is to look at Brazil's past in the wider context of the European colonization of the Americas, though even here Brazil stands out as a unique example because of its Portuguese origins in contrast to Spanish or Anglo-Franco America. Nevertheless, as a European colony, Brazil shared many experiences with struggling Latin and North American nations, most of which achieved their independence in the nineteenth century. In this regard, Brazilian history is a narrative of its people's efforts to assert universal liberties and shape their own destiny and path to progress.

And yet, despite having overthrown the yoke of the Europeans in 1822, the last two hundred years of Brazilian history have been marked by just as much political and socio-economic turmoil. The post-colonial legacy can still be observed in Brazil, as in most, if not all, post-colonial societies. One aspect of Brazilian life today that instantly comes to mind as a clear result of centuries of colonial meddling is the country's diverse ethnocultural makeup. Brazil is a melting pot of Indigenous American, European, and African populations. It also is one of the primary examples of a society where all these different groups managed to integrate seamlessly.

Still, ironically, the main challenges Brazil faces today can be compared to those it faced hundreds of years earlier. Despite the country's significant territorial possessions and vast resources, it is plagued with high levels of social and economic inequality. In the twentieth century, the country underwent significant political changes, including a lengthy military dictatorship, which damaged the integrity of its political structure. To this day, many are skeptical of the country's political and economic elites because of widespread corruption, which also penetrates Brazilian civil services. Ultimately, the problems that shape Brazil today are multifold, and the only way to properly address them is to examine the historical circumstances in which they arose.

Thus, this book offers a concise history of Brazil. In the opening chapters, we will briefly examine the Indigenous societies that dwelled in Brazil before the arrival of European colonizers in the Americas in the late fifteenth century. Unfortunately, our knowledge of this era is mostly limited to European sources and the archeological legacy that remains, which means there is still much more to know about Indigenous Brazilians.

Then, we will move on to the history of Brazil as a colony, from a Portuguese enclave in a Spanish-dominated New World to the largest country in South America. We will examine the economic, political, cultural, and social factors that contributed to the development of Portuguese Brazil. This era laid the foundations of what Brazil would become once it attained independence from the colonizers. We will look at the struggle for independence that transformed the political landscape of Brazil and the entire Western Hemisphere. Finally, the book will tell the story of Brazil's violent and tumultuous shift to democracy from imperialism and the challenges the country had to face since the late nineteenth century. Likewise, we will examine the modern importance of Brazil in Latin American and international political affairs.

Chapter One – The Origins of Colonial Brazil

Age of Exploration

The Late Middle Ages, lasting from roughly the fourteenth to the sixteenth centuries, was a pivotal time in European history—and for good reasons. Politically, the Europeans had managed to reach a somewhat stable status quo, especially in comparison to the previous millennium or so after the fall of Rome in 476. Most kingdoms, such as England or France, had already defined their borders with each other and had established a Christian order with a distinguished social system. They saw the pope as the de facto leader of the Christian world. The expansion of Islam, which had been perhaps the greatest perceived threat to European stability, had mostly been contained.

With the advent of the Ottoman Empire and the fall of Constantinople in 1453, the situation in Europe began to change. Catholic Europe saw an influx of migrants from the former lands of the Byzantine Empire now under the control of the Ottomans. Various scholars, nobles, merchants, and members of the Christian clergy moved to Europe, bringing valuable possessions that included manuscripts of classical antiquity, preserved in the vaults of Greek Churches and previously inaccessible to Western Europeans. This resulted in the renewed will to learn and rediscover the rich classical past of Europe, lost with the chaos that had ensued since the fall of the Western Roman Empire.

This new movement, at first practiced by the richer members of Italian society, would become known as the Renaissance, or "rebirth." The Renaissance, one of the most fundamental products of medieval European thought, was not only concerned with art, literature, and architecture. It also resulted in the development of humanism—a movement that attributed more importance to the capabilities of humans as rational actors who could shape the world they lived in.

In turn, Europeans slowly but surely began studying the world they inhabited. Even as Christianity retained its importance as the chief guide to ordering European life, the humanist movement of the Renaissance made late medieval Europeans hungry for knowledge and understanding. Ironically, the Catholic status quo would eventually be challenged by the Europeans, now increasingly educated in arts, humanities, philosophy, and science. Before the Scientific Revolution of the late sixteenth century and the later Enlightenment movement fundamentally shook up the technological and moral foundations of the continent, however, another development had more immediate material consequences for European kingdoms. It was the beginning of the Age of Exploration.

During the Age of Exploration, also called the Age of Discovery, European nations increasingly undertook more daring voyages, trying to explore what lay beyond the borders of their continent. In hindsight, one might find it strange that the extent of Europe's knowledge of the world was very limited back then. Yes, they knew of faraway places like China and India, having traded with them through intermediary merchants for centuries. Their knowledge of Africa, on the other hand, was mostly limited to the northern coast. From old and new stories, Europe had a rough idea of these distant lands, which it knew produced some of the most valuable materials. Yet, these accounts were often unreliable. In addition, it only became possible to explore the world as the scientific developments of the Renaissance years began to revolutionize navigation and shipbuilding.

At the forefront of European exploration was the Kingdom of Portugal, which began its overseas expansion at the beginning of the fifteenth century. Several factors allowed the Portuguese to undertake such endeavors—circumstances that were simply not true for other Europeans that early. One such factor was Portugal's political landscape at that time, which was very stable and marked with fewer complications. Of course, we must consider that Portugal as a kingdom had been formed after hundreds of years of war against the Muslim dominions of Iberia, which had emerged in the peninsula after the initial stage of Islamic expansion in the eighth century. Portugal was established during the Reconquista, the effort of Christian kings to reclaim Iberia. Since its emergence as an independent kingdom in the twelfth century, Portugal had expanded its territories at the expense of not only Muslims but also neighboring Christian kingdoms. In the late fourteenth century, the kingdom finally cemented its position, with borders close to its modern ones after King John I (Dom João I) became the first ruler of the new Joanine dynasty or House of Aviz.

In fact, the Portuguese policy of overseas expansion was directly influenced by the circumstances created after the monarchy's centralization under the House of Aviz. Different forces began to gain power and influence in the royal court, and all had their own interests and designs for exploration. The monarchy saw overseas expansion as a pragmatic way of boosting the kingdom's income after years of constant wars had significantly depleted the treasury.

Personal enrichment was also the main motivation behind the rising merchant class—a relatively new social class that had emerged as a vital part of Portuguese society.

The Catholic Church, on the other hand, believed that expansion provided an avenue for further spreading God's word and its mission to "heathen" societies. This was especially important for the Portuguese Catholic Church because its history had been shaped by fighting against non-Christian forces.

A lot of commoners were also eager to jump on expeditionary ships and be the first ones into the unknown. For them, especially the male population, it meant the prospect of a new beginning, perhaps one that promised great wealth for those who dared to go on such journeys.

The only major sector of society that was less keen on investing in overseas expansion was the landowning nobility. The nobles enjoyed the status quo and believed that the outpouring of more people in search of new lands to conquer, trading routes to monopolize, and heathens to Christianize acted as a detriment to the labor force on their estates.

The socio-political state of Portugal was thus very important when it came to the early efforts to explore beyond the known parts of the world. However, there were other "enablers" of Portugal's jumpstart in its colonial and expeditionary endeavors.

First, as we mentioned earlier, technological developments in seafaring and navigation allowed for longer and riskier voyages on the high seas. Since the 1440s, the Portuguese increasingly began to use the new caravel ships that were highly mobile and designed to sail in shallow waters, as well. Prince Henry the Navigator (1394-1460), the fourth child of Dom João I whose nickname suggests his active involvement in expeditionary affairs, played a big part. He sponsored many of the initial voyages in exchange for a percentage of the profits the expedition would make. Prince Henry believed that the future of Portugal lay overseas, in whatever form it may have come, partially because the Reconquista had been already completed.

Henry the Navigator.[1]

Overseas expansion was thus perceived as a legitimate way of expanding Portuguese economic and political power. There was also a wider need to find new trade routes to Asia—Europe's longtime supplier of valuable trade materials, especially spices and silk. The expansion of the Ottoman Empire resulted in the monopolization of trade routes by Ottoman merchants, who had close ties with Genoese and Venetian traders. This resulted in the Italians getting a lion's share of the profit by dominating Mediterranean trade coming from the Ottoman Empire. This also contributed to the high level of development of Italian states during the Late Middle Ages.

Before Portugal reached Brazil, however, or even before such long-distance voyages were even perceived to be possible, Portuguese overseas activities were mostly confined to the West African coast. Throughout the fifteenth century, Portuguese expeditions made their way south along the African coast, reaching Cape Bojador in 1434 and, crucially, the Cape of Good Hope in 1487. They did not bother to travel deep into the African continent but instead stuck close to the shore, setting up several trading forts with a permanent small military presence. This meant the Portuguese had a head start in profiting from the goods that flowed out from this part of Africa, most importantly ivory and gold dust.

The Portuguese also held the Atlantic islands close to Europe and Western Africa—Madeira, the Azores, Cape Verde, and São Tomé, which were all acquired throughout the fifteenth century. These islands acted as a reliable network for expanding and concentrating Portuguese trading activities. Each was developed economically to produce profits independently, leading to the establishment of vast sugar plantations. To run the plantations, the Portuguese imported African slaves starting in the mid-fifteenth century, beginning the infamous practice that would shape the socio-political and demographic makeup of the world in a few centuries.

The main objective of finding a reliable maritime trade route through India was accomplished by the end of the century when Vasco da Gama's expedition successfully made its way around the Cape of Good Hope, through the Indian Ocean, into India, and back in 1499. This came as a relief to Portugal for interesting reasons. The obvious one was the fact that the kingdom's main rival—the Kingdom of Castille—was interested in catching up with Portugal's overseas expansion.

Castille had successfully disputed the ownership of the Canary Islands and had imposed its rule upon them early in the fifteenth century. Moreover, in 1492, Queen Isabella I of Castille agreed to fund the expedition of a certain Genoese navigator—Christopher Columbus—who believed he could find a maritime route to India by sailing west instead of south along the African coast. Underestimating the true scale of the circular Earth and unaware of another huge landmass west of Europe beyond the Atlantic, Columbus infamously made his way to the Americas instead of India.

Though offering considerably less than the wealthy lands of China or India, the Caribbean islands that Columbus explored were nevertheless claimed by the Spanish explorers. They provided a valuable outpost from which to organize further voyages onto the American continent, which promised far more riches. When the word of Columbus' first voyage spread throughout Europe after his return in 1493, the Portuguese were quick to expand their efforts, resulting in Vasco da Gama's voyage.

In 1494, Portugal and the Crown of Castille reached an agreement that shaped the future of colonial expansion. It was the adjustment of a papal bull that had granted the Crown of Castille the right to claim the lands west of an arbitrary line drawn 100 leagues west of the Azores. This was partially due to an incorrect interpretation of Columbus' first voyage, which he claimed had reached the China Sea instead of the Antilles in the Caribbean. João II of Portugal renegotiated this papal ruling with Queen Isabelle and King Ferdinand, believing it had unjustly disfavored Portugal. Under the Treaty of Tordesillas, the line was moved a bit more to the west—370 leagues west of the Cape Verde Islands. The lands that would be discovered west of the line could be claimed by Castille, whereas everything east of the line was for Portugal.

The Treaty of Tordesillas itself produced a very arbitrary demarcation, and there was no clear way of knowing which lands would belong to the Portuguese and which to the Spanish. No one was then aware of the size of the Americas, or the fact that India could be reached if one continued west from the point where Columbus had landed. Still, the unknown world promised a lot to the future colonizers.

Soon after Vasco da Gama's return in 1499, another Portuguese expedition, headed by Pedro Álvares Cabral, set sail from Lisbon. Consisting of a fleet of thirteen ships, the expedition—one of the largest of its day—had the goal of reaching the East Indies and setting up Portuguese trading activities there. Instead of sailing south along the African coast, however, the expedition took a westward route after reaching the Cape Verde Islands. About a month later, in late April of 1500, it sighted land and made landfall at Porto Seguro on the eastern coast of Brazil. The Portuguese had made their way to the New World.

Encountering the Natives

The Portuguese arrived in the New World about eight years after the Spanish. And though the two colonial enterprises would eventually take very different shapes, the colonists' initial experiences were largely the same. Besides the fact that the Europeans had no idea what lay in front of them, geographically speaking, another puzzling reality of the exploration and colonization of the New World was encountering the Amerindian population.

The Indigenous population of the Americas was very diverse, even if it could be separated into linguistic or cultural groups—something the Europeans resorted to soon after their arrival. There were two major groups in Brazil when the Portuguese arrived in 1500. The first group was the Tupi-Guarani peoples, who inhabited almost all the Brazilian coast and were the first to come in contact with the Portuguese. The Tupi mostly dwelled in the north, while the Guarani lived in the south. The underlying characteristic and reason behind these peoples' grouping together was their shared language.

The other major group in Brazil identified by the colonizers was the Tapuia—the name used as an umbrella term for all the non-Tupi-Guarani peoples of Brazil. Different tribes in these groups included the Almoré, the Tremembé, and the Goitacá, and they occupied a considerably smaller area than the Tupi-Guarani peoples.

We know little about the Indigenous population of Brazil before the arrival of Europeans. Our knowledge of their origins and ethno-cultural characteristics consists almost entirely of archeological and DNA evidence based on very recent examinations of the territories they inhabited.

The Portuguese produced very biased records against the Natives ever since their first encounters, a problem that generally plagues the narratives of early colonizers. In the writings that have survived from the early stages of colonization, we often see conflicting accounts of Native tribes, mostly based on their relations with the colonizers. Tribes that were friendlier toward the Portuguese and facilitated trade are often referred to positively in contemporary records.

On the other hand, people groups that put up more resistance against the colonizers or those who exhibited cultural characteristics denounced by the Christian way of thought were naturally viewed more negatively. All in all, the early Portuguese interactions with these different peoples produced further prejudices—some lasting for decades. For example, the Aimoré, notorious for their cannibalism (which was practiced by some groups within the Tapuia) and ferocious warfare and military skill were among the most hated Native groups. This prejudice most clearly manifested in 1570 when the ban on enslaving the Natives excluded the

Aimoré.

For certain Indigenous communities, the Portuguese, with their huge ships, powerful weapons, white skin, and Christian practices, were seen as beings capable of possessing special, shamanic powers. Over time, however, as the true intentions of the Portuguese showed themselves, the Natives were forced to adapt to the new circumstances they found themselves in.

The technological superiority of the Portuguese allowed for easy military and political dominance of the Native populations. An effective strategy for the Portuguese was to forge alliances with certain tribes and use them to fight against others, contributing to the development of inter-group fighting and rivalries that eventually undermined the collective Indigenous effort to resist.

Compared to the Portuguese way of life, the social organization of the Natives was more primitive in nearly all aspects. The Indigenous populations lived in small communities and mostly pursued hunter-gatherer activities. They practiced limited, mostly subsistence agriculture and would often migrate from their dwellings once they believed the land could no longer yield crops. Interestingly, the main goods for trade were luxury items such as valuable stones or rare feathers, instead of foodstuffs. These limited trading relations ultimately determined the nature of inter-tribe relations.

The culture of Indigenous Brazilians was rather violent. Cannibalism and sacrifices were prominent practices, reserved exclusively for men, who had greater societal roles than women because they were warriors. However, archeological evidence of the pre-Columbian society of the Marajoara (Marajó) culture, centered on Marajó Island at the mouth of the Amazon River, suggests they bestowed more importance on women. They are often depicted on Marajó pottery, for example.

We will explore the relationship that developed between the colonizers and the Indigenous Amerindians of Brazil in more depth in later chapters. What we will mention here is the obvious and perhaps most horrific legacy of colonization—the decimation of the Indigenous population by diseases brought by the Europeans.

It is difficult to determine the number of Natives that lived in Brazil before the arrival of the Portuguese, with estimates ranging from a few to twelve million Indigenous people. What we can more accurately estimate is that the Indigenous population experienced a complete demographic collapse after encountering diseases for which they had developed no immunity. Smallpox spread rapidly in Indigenous societies, decimating the populations and forcing thousands to migrate inland, which did not stop the severity of the disease's effects. Only about a tenth of the Indigenous Brazilian population was lucky enough to survive after about a century of Portuguese colonization, and the number kept steadily decreasing. The demographic catastrophe brought by Portuguese colonists, coupled with their often ruthless military conquest of Native societies, accelerated the demise of Indigenous communities.

Colonizing Brazil

The first few decades after the arrival of the Portuguese in Brazil were dynamic but not as extensive as Spanish colonial activities at the time, which were centered on exploring Central America. Differently from the Spanish, who dared to venture deep inland from their bases on the Caribbean islands, the Portuguese chose to stick to the coast. They were quick to realize that the land they had reached was vastly different from India. And, since the maritime route to India around Africa had just been discovered, the Portuguese Crown was focused on establishing reliable options to India instead of to an unknown Brazil.

The Portuguese slowly explored the Brazilian coastline while engaging in trade with the Natives, who mainly harvested brazilwood for the colonists in exchange for items that were considered simple and very cheap for the Europeans, like clothing. (The land's name came from the indigenous brazilwood tree, which was not only good for making furniture items but could also be used to produce red dye, making the commodity very important.) Since the Natives already had experience communally harvesting brazilwood in several of their tribes, this relationship was profitable for both sides. This kind of activity continued for about the next three decades.

The Portuguese Crown only began to seriously invest in Brazil's colonization in the 1530s. By that time, Fernando Magellan, a Portuguese sailing under the Spanish flag, had discovered the westward maritime route to India from Europe, which passed through a narrow strait at the southern tip of South America and through the Pacific Ocean. His voyage demonstrated that it would not be a profitable endeavor to develop and pursue this route as a viable alternative to the African route discovered by Vasco da Gama.

This factor, combined with a new external threat, almost convinced the Portuguese Crown to seriously consider extensive colonization of Brazil. The threat came from the French, who had decided to try their luck in colonial endeavors. They had themselves reached the coast of Brazil, which could not be effectively defended by the Portuguese because of its size. In addition, the French did not exactly recognize the Treaty of Tordesillas, believing that it had unjustly and arbitrarily divided the world for the benefit of just two kingdoms, leaving the others out.

Ultimately, when they began to also trade for brazilwood and set up small settlements along the coast in both southern and northern Brazil, Dom João III of Portugal was forced to act. In 1530, recognizing the need for a permanent presence that would defend Portugal's trade interests, he sent an expedition to Brazil, headed by Martim Afonso de Sousa, which was tasked with defending the coastline.

Furthermore, the king decided to implement a more effective administrative system to better control the Portuguese possessions along the coast, dividing it into fifteen units, each ruled by a donatary captain (*donatários*). The captains, who came from diverse social backgrounds, were granted extensive rights over their administrative portions. They effectively ruled the land in the name of the king but did not own it. They collected fees and taxes, were obliged to explore and map their domains and form militias to defend their territories, and could divide the lands among the colonists if they saw it fit.

Yet, the captaincy system provided only a temporary solution to the colonists' problems. Most of the units were not economically successful, for example. The only captaincies that survived and emerged as later centers of Portuguese colonization were Pernambuco in the east and São Vicente in the southeast. Others failed for different reasons, such as the captains' ambitions to overextend and come into conflict with the Natives. The system nevertheless survived in several modified forms until the eighteenth century, with the roles and rights of the captains constantly changing. Significant administrative changes were implemented when Dom João III decided to set up a colonial government in Brazil with a designated governor.

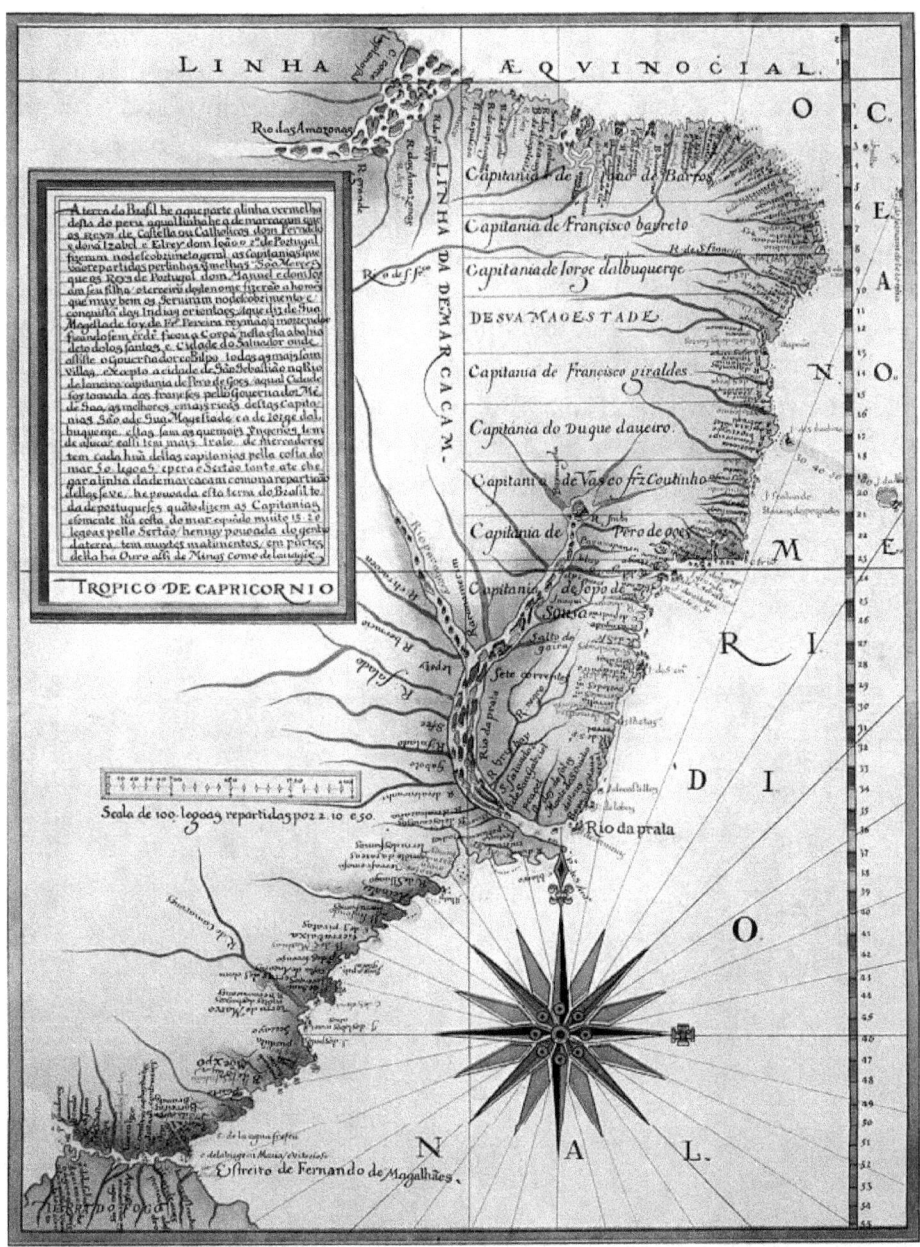

Portuguese map (1574) by Luís Teixeira, showing the location of the hereditary captaincies of Brazil.[2]

This decision was partially influenced by the ongoing success of Spanish colonists in other parts of the Americas. The Spanish had established more effective ways to govern their colonial possessions and had rapidly expanded into Mexico, Central America, and the northwestern part of Southern America. The king, believing that a more centralized form of rule was needed, thus sent Tomé de Sousa to be the first royally appointed governor of Brazil in 1549 with an expedition of about a thousand men. The first governor also brought royal charters that identified the extent of his rights and proceeded to create different administrative positions concerned with judicial matters, the collection of taxes, and the patrol of the coast. There were also Christian missionaries who accompanied de Sousa, including a group of Jesuit priests whose aim it was to strictly monitor the Christian practices of the colonizers.

The new governor and his crew began to set up several large estates, mostly sugar plantations. Sugar would quickly emerge as the main commodity of Brazil aside from brazilwood. Overall, the Crown's hold on the colony became firmer, slowly resulting in economic gains and the development of a system that would last for centuries.

Chapter Two – Portuguese Brazil

Colonial Society

By the mid-sixteenth century, the Portuguese colonial enterprise in Brazil was slowly expanding. Since the Portuguese had committed to staying in their colony long-term, certain social structures began to form—structures that would define Brazil's society for centuries to come. A major aspect of the new society was the system of forced labor that was promptly put in place and grew throughout the years as the economic activity of Portuguese Brazil expanded. The Portuguese not only forced many Natives into slavery but also began to increasingly import enslaved men and women from Africa. This practice eventually became a hugely profitable endeavor in its own right while also among the worst legacies of the age of colonization.

For the colonizers, the decision to transport African slaves to Brazil was very logical. This partially stemmed from the cultural distinctions of Native Brazilian societies. As we mentioned earlier, they were not used to intensive labor and only worked as much as needed to provide for their needs.

This is not to say that the colonists did not enslave the Indigenous population. However, the Natives could also resist strongly, something that further dissuaded the colonists. Many Natives would flee the plantations they were enslaved at, going inland to the Brazilian jungles, which were still unexplored by the Portuguese. Because the Natives were more familiar with the territory they inhabited, they could more effectively run away from the colonists.

Another factor in the shift to African slave labor was the catastrophic collapse of the Native population after their encounter with the Europeans. The contraction of deadly viruses that resulted in the death of most of the Native population simply reduced the available quantity of Natives that could be enslaved by the Portuguese.

The efforts of Christian missionaries, especially the Jesuits, who sought to protect the Natives from slavery, also played a role. However, the Natives were never considered equal to the colonizers, often referred to as objects and non-human "things," even in the writings of religious figures. The Crown's measures, such as outlawing Native enslavement in the 1570s, further contributed, though many of these measures were just as arbitrary. For instance, Natives could still be enslaved if they unjustly attacked the colonizers or practiced cannibalism. Finally, the enslavement of the Indigenous population was fully outlawed in the middle of the eighteenth century, though they already composed a minor portion of Brazil's slave force before this decision.

In the eyes of the Portuguese, Africans were far more suited for the work the colonists required, which included labor-intensive sugar harvesting and refining. Slaves that were transported from Africa were also less prone to developing such deadly responses to European diseases as the Indigenous Amerindians. Though many of them died soon after arriving in Brazil, there were more of them to enslave.

The Portuguese had actively pursued the slave trade for about a century and knew how profitable it could be. By the first half of the seventeenth century, when sugar production reached its peak, so did the rate at which the Portuguese transported African slaves to Brazil. The numbers grew exponentially. It is estimated that before slavery was outlawed in the middle of the nineteenth century, as many as four million African slaves had been brought to Brazil—mostly young males who died within the first few years of arriving in South America.

The growth of Portuguese colonial activities in Brazil went hand in hand with the growth of the practice of slavery. Certain port cities, such as Rio de Janeiro and Salvador, the capital of Brazil until the middle of the eighteenth century, became centers of the Brazilian slave trade. Portuguese connections and possessions on the African coast allowed for large-scale slave trade, an enterprise in which Portugal was the leading European nation and would remain so for centuries.

The Africans who were enslaved came from diverse ethnic backgrounds. This was a deliberate practice as the colonists believed that transporting many Africans from the same communities would incite resistance movements among the slaves once they were transported to Brazil. This, combined with the vastness of the Brazilian territory and the African slaves' unfamiliarity with it, proved effective against any efforts of united resistance against the colonists.

Still, instances of runaway African slaves were common, and they would often organize communities, known as the *quilombos*, where they would establish their Indigenous practices. Though not always large, these communities were located in the peripheries of Portuguese control. Sometimes they would grow by allowing convicted and wanted white or Indigenous Amerindians to join.

Slaves made up the lowest social stratum of Brazilian colonial society, where divisions were primarily based on ethnicity and social background. This characteristic was present in all American colonial societies in different shapes and forms. White male colonists, especially those born in Portugal, were favored among the rest of the population, having access to full rights based on their social role.

The diffusion of Europeans, Indigenous groups, and Africans eventually resulted in different ethnic-based classes, such as the mulatto class, which ultimately made up most of the population in the biggest Brazilian cities. The cafusos, the name given to those with a mixture of Indigenous and African ancestry, occupied a lower position in the social hierarchy, though they were technically considered "free." It is important to understand that white colonists were always at a numerical disadvantage, especially in large urban centers such as Rio de Janeiro. Because most of the colonists were males (especially in the first decades of colonization), intermarriage and sexual intercourse with the Indigenous people was a common practice.

Prejudices about the "natural" or "God-given" inferiority of different ethnic groups held by the white colonists were supported by prominent institutions, such as the Catholic Church. Later, with the development of pseudoscientific beliefs that bestowed false importance on the physical characteristics of Africans or Indigenous people, many of these prejudices would be reinforced. According to their adherents, features such as the size of the skull or the "density" of the brain proved their inferiority to white people. These deterministic beliefs greatly influenced the makeup of

Brazilian society and the social roles adopted by the different groups within it for centuries to come. Structural exploitation of those believed to have been "naturally inferior" produced further divisions that can still be observed in most post-colonial societies, including in Brazil.

Of course, there were also social distinctions within the different ethnic classes. The colonists aimed to shape Brazilian society according to European models and standards, copying the functions of the prominent social classes of medieval Portugal as closely as possible. This included the distinctions between members of the nobility, the clergy, and commoners. However, these distinctions were not as pronounced in Brazil.

Few nobles from Portugal abandoned their possessions and influence in Europe and entirely relocated to the colony because of the obvious risks associated with this move. Members of colonial society who were descendants of Portuguese nobility were referred to as *fidalgos* and were more respected than self-made colonists who had accrued great wealth by being the first to undertake colonial endeavors.

The differences in the medieval Portuguese *ancien regime* only became more prominent in the nineteenth century when the Portuguese royal family was forced to flee Lisbon and come to Brazil in exile. This defining moment in Brazilian history, and the social and political circumstances it gave rise to, will be covered in greater detail in later chapters.

Before then, the top positions in the social hierarchy were occupied by those who had the most economic power—wealthy landowners and merchants. The social movements during the Renaissance had already increased the standing of merchants in European societies, out of which a distinct upper-middle class began to form. Since they were instrumental in providing the means to transport goods to the motherland and keep the colony economically viable, their importance in the colonies grew even more.

The richest members of the landowning class, on the other hand, were plantation owners who produced sugar in large quantities thanks to the slave labor they employed. Most of the planters were not of noble origin. Instead, this group was comprised of those who had been the first to set up plantations in Brazil.

The planters and the merchants maintained a firm grip over the colonial society of Brazil. They were the driving forces behind its economy, and it was in their chief interests for the status quo to continue. Still, the two came into conflict with each other at times since their respective powers could not effectively be checked by government authorities.

Brazilian Economy

The basic organizing principle behind the colonial economic activities in Portuguese Brazil was mercantilism. Most, if not all, European nations at the time pursued a mercantilist policy, maintaining that each nation must accumulate as many resources as it could by limiting imports and relying on exports. This principle was true of the Portuguese, who saw their overseas territories, Brazil included, as a means of supplying the mother country with valuable resources that could be exported to foreign markets. In fact, diversifying the resources available to each nation was one of the main agendas of colonization. To pursue this goal and dominate international trade, European monarchies heavily regulated domestic economic activities—and Portugal was no exception.

In 1571, for example, the Portuguese Crown adopted a policy that would shape the economic activity in Brazil for centuries to come. Resources produced in Brazil were to be exclusively accessed by Portuguese merchants and traded to Portugal. No foreign merchants were allowed to approach Brazilian ports. Portuguese merchants, who had to pay a tax on goods imported to the Crown, were paying as little as possible for goods and then artificially inflating their prices when selling them. This approach, in the long term, was detrimental to colonial economies, which, despite producing huge quantities of resources for the mother countries, were unjustly compensated. The Crown, however, encouraged mercantilism by supporting the creation of state-funded and semi-private trading companies that specialized in trade with the colonies and extracted as much as they could.

The policy that granted exclusive rights to Portuguese merchants to access trade in Brazil, implemented in 1571, followed several decades of freedom of trade. To ensure that the merchants would follow the policy, the Crown needed to establish firm control over its possessions in Brazil and maintain a public order in which individuals were reminded that they were still subjects of the Portuguese monarchy. This had been one of the main goals behind the establishment of a governorship.

Additionally, public order and obedience to the Crown were guaranteed thanks to the role of the Catholic Church and the increasing presence of religious figures in Brazil, who were especially prominent from the middle of the sixteenth century. Catholic missionaries were eager to spread Catholicism, the state religion of Portugal, partially because they perceived Protestant Christian missionaries as their direct rivals. The Church and the state thus developed a mutually beneficial relationship surrounding their roles in Brazil, especially in the early days of colonization. The Crown defended the clergy and often granted it lands to set up monasteries in the colony. Through its constant involvement in the everyday life of the Brazilian-Portuguese subjects, the Church was a guarantor of order and had a free hand in spreading Catholicism. It also paid a portion of its earnings to the Crown.

The economic output of Brazil was diverse, with regions specializing in the production of different goods. At first, the northeastern part of the colony was the most important economically, stemming from the fact that it was the first area colonized by the Portuguese. The coastal city of Salvador, now in the modern-day state of Bahia, was the capital of the colony until 1763, stimulating growth and production around the city.

This part of the colony depended on the production and export of sugar, one of the most valuable commodities in the world in the sixteenth and seventeenth centuries. A century earlier, it had become a staple of European cuisine instead of a luxury product. The colonists soon set up a system that maximized sugar production. Aided by a very suitable climate for growing sugar, Brazil experienced an economic boom during these years. The northeastern captaincies profited the most, thanks in part to their relative proximity to European ports and rich soil that was irrigated by the Amazon River.

The Crown aided the development of the sugar economy in Brazil by, for example, exempting sugar planters from paying additional taxes on their earnings. This incentivized more and more people to plant sugar even though sugar harvesting was a tenuous, labor-intensive, and intricate process requiring great skill, perfect conditions, and adequate equipment. Because of the expensive nature of sugar production, planters usually borrowed money from all sorts of creditors, including religious institutions and independent Catholic orders that enjoyed special financial privileges. Later, planters developed a symbiotic relationship with wealthy merchants, who often financed the establishment of sugar plantations and, in turn, purchased sugar from the planters at a reduced price.

By the late sixteenth century, efforts to encourage sugar production also had the indirect effect of increasing the number of African slave laborers who worked on the plantations. Processing sugar required intensive labor, which, in turn, took a physical toll on those who worked in the fields. Since the Portuguese colonists viewed African slaves as essentially disposable resources, they increasingly relied on them to harvest sugar. This resulted in the deaths of tens of thousands of slaves, many of whom, as we mentioned earlier, died from overworking or horrific living conditions.

Since the demand for African slaves increased during this period, more and more slaves were transported from Portugal's African holdings to Brazil, and their prices began to rise, as well. Many planters, who had greatly increased their wealth and influence by the middle of the seventeenth century, could afford more and more slaves, further increasing their profits.

Brazil essentially held a monopoly in sugar production and almost single-handedly supplied European markets for decades until other colonies increasingly began to harvest sugar themselves. The Caribbean colonies of France and England emerged as the main competitors for Brazil.

Although Brazil's economic output increasingly diversified in the later decades of the seventeenth century as a response to the new rivals, sugar nevertheless remained a central product. Sugar made up about half of all Brazilian exports in the eighteenth century, though its profitability had greatly decreased from its heyday a century and a half earlier. Later, international factors like the slave rebellion in the French colony of Saint Domingue (Haiti)— the largest sugar producer in the world at the time— revived the profitability of Brazilian sugar. The rebellion, which turned into a full-on revolution in Haiti, greatly disrupted sugar production on the island and incentivized merchants to visit neighboring colonial markets to buy sugar.

Cotton, tobacco, brazilwood, coffee, and manioc were also among the goods produced in Brazil. Domestically, many landowners also began to raise cattle, which became a vital part of the Brazilian agricultural market. Crucially, at the end of the seventeenth century, gold was discovered in the southern parts of Brazil, inciting a gold rush. Gold, for obvious reasons, quickly became the main Brazilian export alongside sugar and greatly contributed to the development of southern Brazil, which had previously been considered a periphery. It also motivated the colonists to move deeper inland and explore the mysterious hinterlands of Brazil, resulting in the founding of new settlements. The Brazilian gold rush ultimately shaped the socio-economic dynamics of the colony in the eighteenth century, which we will explore in greater detail later.

Crisis in Brazil

Throughout the sixteenth century, Brazil thus began to develop into an important overseas possession of Portugal. Though it could not boast the abundance of precious metals that were present in Spain's American colonies, it nevertheless gradually expanded its economic output, attracting notice from the motherland. More and more colonists began to emigrate to Portuguese Brazil. The coastline was studied very well, and several expeditions even journeyed into the interior with hopes of finding more wealth.

It was between the sixteenth and the seventeenth centuries that Portuguese possessions in Brazil began to face their first significant threat. This stemmed from the complex international political climate that emerged in the late 1500s as the European kingdoms engaged in continent-wide conflicts that also affected their overseas territories.

In 1578, the Portuguese monarchy experienced a succession crisis after the death of King Sebastian I, who left no heirs. His great-uncle Henry, a cardinal of the Catholic Church, ruled the kingdom for the next two years. But after he died in 1580, the Crown was left without an heir once again. Different contenders emerged for the Portuguese throne, but the nobility chose Spain's King Philip II as the new king. This resulted in the establishment of the Iberian Union—about sixty years during which the Spanish branch of the House of Habsburg ruled Spain (itself a union of the crowns of Castille and Aragon) and Portugal. The Habsburg rulers had also inherited possessions in Italy and the Netherlands, making them the most powerful dynasty in Europe at the time.

The Iberian Union meant that the Spanish and the Portuguese could temporarily disregard the line of the Tordesillas Treaty, the century-old agreement that was still respected by the two. Interested parties from both kingdoms, most importantly wealthy merchants and colonists in the Americas, hoped to gain easier access to previously unexplored markets and profit from the new political situation.

During this period, several large-scale expeditions into the heart of South America were first organized by the Portuguese, who crossed the arbitrary border set by the Treaty of Tordesillas and ventured into the Amazon. Though no permanent large settlements were established in what became the central-westernmost part of modern-day Brazil, the state of Mato Grosso, these expeditions provided valuable leverage for the Portuguese to claim the unexplored South American lands.

On the other hand, being in a personal union with the Spanish Crown meant that the Portuguese were also drawn into the conflicts fought by the Spanish Habsburgs. At the time, the Spanish Crown was facing a rebellion from its subjects in the Netherlands—a conflict that had begun in the 1560s and would eventually last until the middle of the seventeenth century. Covering intricate details of the Dutch Revolt against the Spanish Habsburgs is beyond the scope of this book, but what we do need to establish is that the Dutch, having colonial designs, began to attack Portuguese possessions in Africa, Asia, and South America. They raided Salvador in 1604 and were a menacing threat to Portuguese ships in the Atlantic for the next few years.

Despite a twelve-year truce between the Spanish and the Dutch from 1609 to 1621 during which the Portuguese colony enjoyed a brief period of peace, the Dutch began to increasingly eye Portuguese territories in South America. Attracted by the lucrative sugar industry, the Dutch created the Dutch West India Company to gain control of the weakly defended colonies in South America and emerge as the new colonial superpower. In Asia, the Dutch East Indies Company pursued similar goals against Portugal's Asian colonies.

Three years after the truce was broken, in 1624, the Dutch attacked Salvador again and occupied it without much resistance. The attack came as another shock to the Portuguese colonists in Brazil, who fled Salvador and utilized guerilla tactics for the next few months to keep the Dutch forces from expanding their control beyond the city. It was only in May of 1625, after the arrival of a force of more than 10,000 soldiers from Europe, that the Dutch surrendered Salvador and gave control of the city back to the Portuguese.

In 1630, the Dutch returned with a new force, now attacking northeastern Brazil and taking the coastal cities of Recife and Olinda. This time, the Portuguese were unable to drive the Dutch back so quickly due to the help they received from local Portuguese colonists. The Dutch West India Company established its headquarters in Recife and slowly began to conquer the coastal territories further to the north. What emerged was Dutch Brazil, or, as the Dutch themselves referred to the colony, New Holland. Portuguese guerilla fighters nevertheless made it difficult for the Dutch to profit from sugar production for the next few years.

The struggle for control of northeastern Brazil would continue until 1654. By then, Portugal was no longer in a personal union with the Spanish Crown, and the Dutch had finally gained their independence from the Habsburgs after eighty years of fighting. However, the Portuguese still intended to take back what they had lost to the Dutch in the 1630s.

Thanks to resistance efforts from local leaders such as João Fernandes Vieira and André Vidal de Negreiros, Portuguese colonists in Brazil began to achieve small victories over the Dutch positions. The center of the insurrection against the Dutch was the rural area of Pernambuco, and the victories eventually reduced Dutch holdings to Recife. The locals emerged victorious in the two decisive battles of Guararapes in 1648 and 1649, further weakening the position of the Dutch in Brazil.

In early 1652, due to the growing tensions between the Netherlands and England over their possessions in North America, the two states went to war, taking a tremendous toll on the Dutch war effort in Brazil. At this pivotal moment, King João VI of Portugal finally decided to send a large naval squadron to expel the Dutch from Recife once and for all. They surrendered to the Portuguese forces in January of 1654.

Consolidation and Expansion

The war against the Dutch highlighted obvious problems that had existed in the colonial system. The inability to defend key coastal cities from Dutch assaults made it clear that Portugal had long ignored the defense of its valuable colony. Though the Crown ultimately reacted to the invasion and occupation of Brazil by the Dutch forces, victory was ultimately thanks to the efforts of locals. Moreover, the Dutch had also briefly occupied the Portuguese possessions in Africa, in modern-day Angola. This had partially disrupted the influx of African slaves to Brazil and had further hindered stabilization after the war. All in all, Portugal's economy took a great hit during the middle of the seventeenth century, and the country barely retained control of Brazil, where the colonizers were eager to resume imperial exploitation for material gains.

Still, increasing efforts had been made since the late sixteenth century to further explore the Brazilian interior. The obvious route was up the Amazon River in the northern part of the country. No one knew the extent of the rainforests, let alone the path the river took before its mouth opened at the Atlantic Ocean. Exploring this part of the continent promised to be a worthy endeavor because it could potentially link the Portuguese possessions with the Spanish colonies in the northern and western parts of South America. The coastal town of Belém, founded in 1616 at the mouth of the Amazon, served this purpose and was a point of resistance against the French, who occupied lands further north (territories that eventually became French Guiana).

In 1637, Portuguese explorer Pedro Teixeira became the first European to successfully journey the whole length of the Amazon River, reaching Spanish Peru and claiming the vast lands of the Amazon jungle for the Portuguese colony in the process. This part of Brazil, now organized into the states of Para and Amazonas, remained underdeveloped, however, with a large concentration of Indigenous people. It could not specialize in large-scale agricultural production, such as the cultivation of sugar or cotton, was very poor, and was still very unexplored.

The dense tropical rainforests dissuaded most explorers from trying their luck in the area, but not all feared leading expeditions deeper inland—especially those with a divine mission to spread the word of God. Yes, the effort to explore northern and central Brazil was spearheaded by Christian missionaries, especially the Jesuit groups, who began founding small villages and converted tens of thousands of indigenous Amerindians to Catholicism by the middle of the eighteenth century.

Overall, the Jesuits were against the systemic violence practiced against Indigenous people, and the colonists sometimes viewed them unfavorably for this reason. Since they had obtained support from the Indigenous people, many saw their growing influence in the region as potentially damaging to the future cohesion of the colony. Consequently, the Jesuits were temporarily expelled from the area in 1684. They eventually returned and continued missionary activities until 1752, when the Crown banned their activities in northern Brazil.

Early efforts had also been made to expand south, where the city of São Paulo had been founded in 1554 by a group of Jesuit missionaries. Named after Paul the Apostle and located on a convenient plateau about 800 meters above sea level, São Paulo, acted as a center from which missions were launched for the first several decades of its existence. The main reason for this was, again, the larger presence of Indigenous groups. In fact, the northern and southernmost regions of Brazil were similar in many other ways as well. Both regions had a weaker economic output and a stronger influence of Jesuit missionaries. Portuguese colonists often intermarried with the Natives, giving rise to the *mameluco* class, a word used to refer to the offspring of white colonists and Natives.

São Paulo also acted as an important center for further exploration to the south and west. Expeditionary settlers were referred to as *bandeirantes*. The name comes from the Portuguese word for flag— *bandeira*—as the expeditions were headed by designated flag bearers and old Portuguese military units containing up to fifty men. The *bandeirantes* played a very important role in the expansion of colonial Brazil's borders well beyond the line of Tordesillas. Their expeditions were made up of local Paulista (residents of São Paulo) *mamelucos*, and white colonists, who were in charge. The expeditions were supported by large numbers of Indigenous Amerindians, who followed the colonists' lead and were instrumental in navigating the unknown areas of southern Brazil.

A painting of Brazilian bandeirantes.[3]

The *bandeirantes* journeyed in all directions from São Paulo, regularly encountering previously uncontacted villages of Natives and enslaving the Indigenous population. Their expeditions sometimes took several years to complete, and many of them were organized independently from the colonial government's support. Of course, the Portuguese bureaucrats in charge of the São Vicente captaincy and beyond generally welcomed the *bandeirantes'* efforts to explore the remote areas, especially since they further spread Portuguese control over the Native-dominated areas.

Imprisoned Amerindians from these remote villages were mostly sold as slaves in the south, mostly in Rio de Janeiro, where there was a new demand for slave labor due to the recent development of the sugar industry. Extensive *bandeirante* activities coincided with the years when the steady supply of African slaves to Brazil was disrupted due to the ongoing war with the Dutch.

Bandeirante expeditions were also vital to the history of colonial Brazil in another aspect. In the late seventeenth century, in the modern-day mountainous state of Minas Gerais, the *bandeirantes* discovered gold. As one can imagine, this greatly affected the socio-economic dynamics of colonial Brazil, prompting a gold rush that led thousands of colonists to undertake journeys into the unknown in search of the precious metal. This was especially true for many who came directly from Portugal to southern Brazil in search of new and prosperous lives. It is estimated that more than half a million Portuguese came to Brazil during the first few decades after the discovery of gold.

This discovery fueled the economy of the southern part of the colony, which had previously been overshadowed by the richer sugar-producing areas in the northeast. Now, however, the northeast slowly began to lose its economic and political importance. Sugar production had already been hit hard during the wars with the Dutch, and the rising demand for slave labor and increasing emigration to the south had their consequences. This was best manifested in 1763, when the colony's capital was transferred from Salvador to Rio de Janeiro, which quickly became the fastest-growing city in Brazil alongside São Paulo.

Another effect of the discovery of gold was that the Portuguese Crown became more interested in regulating its colony, leading to the establishment of new administrative demarcations and important civil services, such as town tribunals and courts. Gold was also heavily taxed, with at least a fifth of all mined precious metals (diamond was also discovered but in a much smaller quantity) going directly to the royal treasury. Colonist miners were also taxed based on the amount of slaves they employed. Those who were independent, meaning they had no slaves, also had to pay additional fees.

The extent to which the motherland suddenly became involved in the everyday life of colonial Brazil was remarkable. The Crown also tried to balance the interests of different regions of its colony. The inhabitants of São Paulo had initially requested special privileges regarding access to gold mines, but it was not in the interest of Lisbon to openly favor one part of the colony over another. Quotas for slaves were introduced in the south to make sure that slave supply to the northeastern sugar plantations remained stable.

Yet, such rapid and active involvement in the affairs of the newest colonial region had its consequences. Both European and *mameluco* colonists began to distrust centrally appointed authorities, who increasingly disregarded their demands in order to accrue as much profit for the Crown as possible. With the mining economy growing thanks to the increased supply of slaves, the wealthiest colonists in the southern region gained much influence and political power. Many wealthy landowners, some of them sugar planters, also diversified their incomes by becoming involved in the mining business.

The discovery of gold also contributed to the development of new sectors of the economy centered on gold, creating opportunities for directly extracting the resource. This reached its peak in the middle of the eighteenth century and slowly began to decline, with Brazilian gold mines gradually running dry by the nineteenth century.

Chapter Three – The Birth of Independent Brazil

Wrestling with the Motherland

A period of true social and political turbulence began in Brazil in the second half of the eighteenth century. At the core of this upheaval were, once again, broader international developments in Europe that forever transformed the fate of the continent and its people. The absolutist monarchic structure of European kingdoms and empires began to show its cracks as the Age of Enlightenment brought new ideas about self-governance and personal liberties. Major British and French thinkers challenged the absolutist status quo with their writings, asserting the fundamental principles of liberalism upon which the modern Western world would eventually be founded.

These liberal ideas manifested in a series of crises experienced by some of the most powerful European empires, resulting in the outbreak of the Thirteen Colonies' war of independence from Great Britain in 1776. The revolutionaries defeated the British forces, founding the United States of America, which posed a threat to the imperial designs of the Europeans. In addition, the French Revolution, which began in 1789, brought a significant paradigm shift in Europe. With the French King Louis XVI overthrown, the revolutionaries proclaimed a republic and proceeded to implement radical measures that threatened other monarchies around the continent.

Hand in hand with these political developments were socio-economic shifts. The Industrial Revolution ushered in an era of previously unseen economic development thanks to the invention of new machinery and the use of new sources of energy to perform labor. The development of local factories boosted the productivity of European industry and manufacturing, resulting in higher levels of urbanization that positively impacted economic development.

The events of the mid-to-late eighteenth century and the ideas they were based on had their foundation in the breakthroughs in science and philosophy during the Renaissance, which had also kickstarted the Age of Discovery that had made certain European powers masters of the New World. Now, however, these same ideas, further developed (and, in some cases, radicalized), posed a threat to the same colonial possessions.

In the ever-changing Western world, Portugal was a clear loser. Compared to France, and, especially, Britain—which had spearheaded the Industrial Revolution and gotten a head start in economic development—Portugal greatly lagged.

The British, who were rapidly industrializing and adopting new economic policies to ensure further growth of their domestic and overseas markets, tried to exploit the weakness of Portugal's and Spain's colonial possessions. They also began to abandon their long-standing mercantilist practices and started to practice free trade. Even after having lost their possessions in North America in the American Revolutionary War, the British were slowly emerging as the new hegemon of the world. Their relatively stable political system allowed them to dominate their rivals overseas. They were increasingly involved in the economic activities of other European colonies, which still followed the principles of exclusivity that put local merchants at a disadvantage. The British often secretly negotiated with foreign merchants to gain access to their markets, encouraging smuggling and other illegal activities that damaged the colonial incomes of Spain and Portugal.

The Portuguese, on the other hand, tried to keep up with the rapidly modernizing world, though they were reluctant to completely abandon the *ancien regime*. Although they began to take measures to rival the British with the reforms undertaken during the reign of Dom José I, they were too late. By the late eighteenth century, Brazil's gold mines were starting to run dry, and the emergence of other large sugar manufacturers caused an economic crisis in the colony. Back in Portugal, Lisbon had almost completely been destroyed by a massive earthquake in 1755, and funds were directed toward rebuilding the capital. In South America, Portuguese explorers were increasingly clashing with the Spanish over the southern territories, which put a further toll on the kingdom.

As a response, the Crown tried to further centralize its rule over the colonies and gain firmer control over its economic output. For example, as we mentioned, the Crown decided to expel the Jesuits from Brazil in 1759. The possessions of the religious order were confiscated and either completely seized or redistributed. Factories were also set up in the urban areas of Brazil to incentivize local production and not be completely reliant on raw materials as the main source of income for Brazil's economy. Portugal also encouraged efforts to further integrate the Indigenous population into colonial society, politically dominated by white colonists and mixed-race individuals. To this end, the Crown abolished Indigenous slavery in 1757, as mentioned earlier.

Yet, these measures were not enough to significantly change the socio-economic landscape in Brazil, where many began to blame their problems on their colonial overlords. Brazilians closely observed the developments in other European colonies, especially in the United States, which was an example of successful resistance against colonial powers and the assertion of the right of self-governance. Liberal ideas motivated groups to organize local conspiracy movements in different regions of Brazil. Though these movements laid the foundation for a national consciousness that later resulted in Brazilian independence, they were not widely supported in the colony. The dominant classes of colonial Brazil, including wealthy landowners and merchants, largely supported maintaining the status quo of social inequality, though they also believed that independence from Portugal could greatly increase their personal gains.

Out of the late eighteenth-century conspiracies in Brazil, the Inconfidência Mineira stands out the most. Its leaders, the *inconfidentes*, were members of the Minas Gerais elite and included several rich landowners, colonial military and government officials, lawyers, and businessmen who had ties with both the colonial regime in Brazil and Europe. Influenced by the prominent liberal ideas of the time, they recognized the declining social state of their region, plagued by economic crises and corruption. Their goal was to overthrow the colonial government and organize a constitutional republic modeled after the United States. The separatists supported the abolition of slavery in Brazil and the subsequent creation of an egalitarian, independent society.

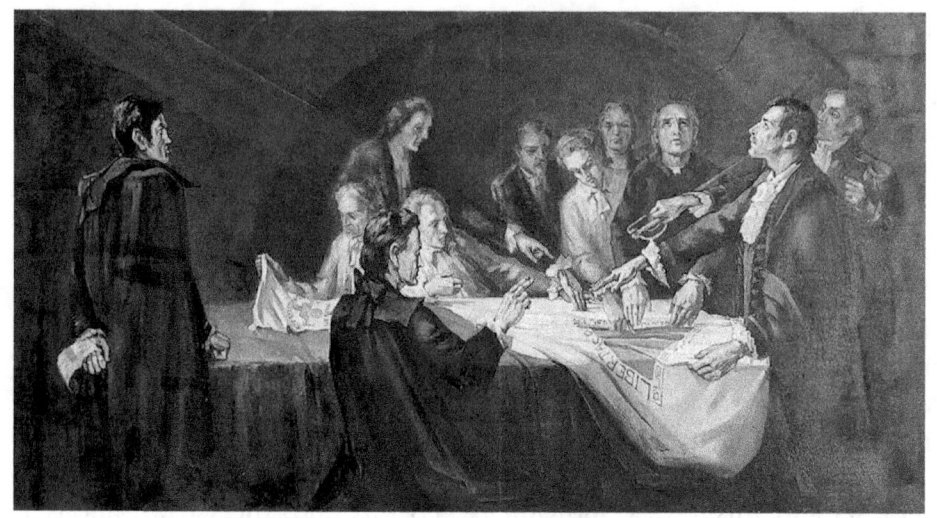
The inconfidentes by Carlos Oswald.'

Despite developing plans as early as 1788, the *inconfidentes* were never able to act, and their conspiracy was soon discovered. Imprisoned and trialed for the next couple of years, they were sentenced to death by hanging in 1792. The body of one of their members, a low-ranking military officer named Joaquim José da Silva Xavier—better known by his nickname *Tiradentes*, or "Tooth Puller"—was cut to pieces after the execution, and his head was put on public display at the town square of Ouro Preto. Though the Inconfidência Mineira did not materialize into any gains for the local Brazilians against the Portuguese colonizers, the symbolic importance of the movement remained in the colonists' consciousness. Eventually, Tiradentes, who had claimed responsibility for leading the insurrection despite playing a relatively small part in it, became a national hero of independent Brazil. As a martyr who died for freedom, he still lives on in the memory of Brazilians.

Monarchy in Brazil

The beginning of the nineteenth century brought another unique development, influenced by the circumstances in Europe, that greatly affected the future of Brazil. Having emerged as the emperor of France after the chaos of the French Revolution, Napoleon Bonaparte waged a war against most of Europe in the first decade of the 1800s. The success of the French in the early stages of the Napoleonic Wars had resulted in their total domination of Western Europe and an economic embargo on Great Britain—Napoleon's main adversary and the only power he could not decisively defeat. The Continental System, set up in 1806, prohibited any of France's European client states from trading with the British. The system was enforced by the French, though some countries, such as Russia, still secretly practiced trade with Great Britain.

Another exception to the blockade was Portugal, which had so far remained neutral in the wars against France and had been defensively allied with the British. Believing that the trade between the British and the Portuguese endangered his goals in Europe, the French general decided to invade Portugal through his client state of Spain in November 1807.

Portugal was not prepared for an all-out war against the French, and not only because of the superiority of the veteran French forces. The Crown was also in a political crisis at the time. The ruling Queen Maria I, who had experienced the deaths of her husband, Dom Peter III, and her son and heir to the throne, Prince Joseph, had developed problems with her mental state and could not effectively govern the kingdom. In her stead, rulership had been assumed by her younger son, Prince João, who would become Dom João VI of Portugal in 1816 after his mother's death.

Acting as regent in the most critical period of the throne, the young prince knew he could not put up a fight against Napoleon's French war machine. Instead, he made the very interesting decision to flee Portugal to Brazil.

Upon hearing of the French invasion, João, escorted by the British armada, decided to transfer the royal court to Rio de Janeiro, leaving the kingdom in Europe free for Napoleon's taking. In late November of 1807, the young prince, accompanied by some 15,000 people, including state bureaucrats and officials, members of the royal family, judges, nobility, important religious figures, and army and naval officers, set sail for South America.

João VI of Portugal.[5]

In a move that shocked the Portuguese population, the prince took everything he deemed valuable for the functioning of the Crown to deny

35

the French control over the Portuguese government apparatuses. This included the royal treasury, printing presses, and royal archives. People were right in thinking that their suzerain had abandoned them, cowardly fleeing a confrontation with Napoleon's forces. João and his court had tried to tell his subjects to remain calm and not resist the invaders, saying that the royal family would one day return, though this did little to dissuade the panic.

The journey to Brazil was long and tenuous. Overcrowding in the ships was a major problem, causing a shortage of supplies and poor sanitary conditions that resulted in the outbreak of several diseases and many deaths. The ships also greatly suffered from storms in the Atlantic that separated parts of the navy and created organizational problems. Finally, João and most of the ships arrived in Salvador, rather than Rio, where the prince's mother and other members of the royal family were transported. The reason behind the change of destination is unclear, though it was probably done to assert the political significance of the old capital. His court only briefly stayed in Salvador, however, continuing the journey to Rio in about a month and beginning a new era in the history of Brazil.

The transfer of the monarchy to Brazil was a unique instance in the history of European colonization and was followed by significant social and political developments in Rio and elsewhere. Many problems needed to be addressed in Brazil, some of them brought by the thousands of new immigrants and others rooted in the historical development of the colony. One of the first measures of Prince João's administration was to open the Brazilian ports to foreign ships—a decree that aimed to normalize trade relations with Britain.

Witnessing the ongoing situation in Brazil prompted the prince's administration to adopt other significant changes directed at boosting Brazil's economy. The Crown began to support the Brazilian economy by directly investing in the creation of factories to boost local manufacturing and providing subsidies for different industries. Many tariffs, part of the old mercantilist system, were abolished to encourage domestic and international trade.

Though these changes brought positive improvements to Brazil, the British benefitted the most, economically speaking. João's decrees essentially legalized trade with the British merchants, who had practiced contraband trade in Brazilian ports for many decades. The fate of Portugal as an independent kingdom in Europe was largely dependent on

Great Britain and its war against the French, a reality that gave the British a lot of political influence. A part of the British Royal Navy also defended Brazil's coast in case of a foreign invasion, as the Portuguese Crown had no resources to muster up a competent navy. The British used this influence to strike even more profitable agreements with the Portuguese in Brazil, guaranteeing advantages for British products that flowed into Brazil's ports.

On the other hand, it soon became clear to many Brazilians that the royal court's residence in Brazil did not exactly mean prosperity. The Crown was still acting in its own interests and largely disregarding the demands of the local population. Because effective control over the European territories had been lost, Brazilians were now overtaxed. And, as mentioned earlier, freedom from trade restrictions did not alleviate the new tax burden. Additionally, some of the measures taken by Prince João resulted in further instability. He organized several military expeditions to the south with the hopes of gaining control over Banda Oriental on the River Plate, where the Portuguese had contested Spanish claims for over a century.

This discontent with the new regime was best manifested in the Pernambuco rebellion of 1817, during which the entire northeastern province revolted against the newly crowned Dom João VI. The rebels blamed the king for favoring not only the Portuguese members of his kingdom over the locals but also the southern Brazilians over the northerners. A strong regional identity had been a staple of Pernambuco, and it is no surprise that the movement against the Crown in 1817 was very heterogeneous, with most sectors of Pernambuco's society participating in the revolt. Beginning from the city of Recife, the revolt eventually spread to other parts of Brazil, making it the first significant threat to Dom João's safety since his arrival in Brazil. However, the diverse composition of the rebellion also meant that the different groups had joined the movement to pursue their own ends, destabilizing the whole effort. The royal forces were thus subdued the rebellion in May and executed its leaders in Recife.

From a Colony to an Empire

By then, the Napoleonic Wars had ended with the defeat of the French, and the antebellum status quo was restored in Europe. The victors pushed for the strengthening of conservative monarchies on the continent. This meant that Dom João and his court could return to

Portugal and rule the colony from there. However, João decided to stay in Brazil, choosing to inaugurate the former colony into a united kingdom with its former colonial motherland. What resulted was the Kingdom of Portugal, Brazil and the Algarves—a union in which the overseas territories of Portugal were at least nominally equal in status.

The new kingdom was short-lived, however. Dom João's decision to stay in Brazil with his court had seemed strange to the Portuguese in Europe, and so did the proclamation of a new union with Brazil and the Algarves. In 1820, a military uprising in the city of Porto resulted in the outbreak of a liberal revolution in Portugal, with the revolutionaries setting up a junta government and ruling in the name of the king. The aim of the revolution, inspired by the liberal ideas of the Enlightenment, was to address the ongoing ambiguity in Portugal with the absence of the king and other government entities.

Though the revolutionaries were against the institution of absolute monarchy, the nature of the revolution was not fully "liberal," as they supported Portugal's control over its overseas territories. This was characteristic of other liberal movements around the same time. During the Haitian Revolution a few decades earlier, for example, many French liberals had advocated for the French army to quell the rebellion and retake control over Haiti, which provided mainland France with valuable resources and was a driving force behind its economy. The Portuguese revolutionaries mostly thought along the same lines in 1820.

The revolutionaries also decided to call for the convention and reformation of the Cortes. The Cortes was an old Portuguese assembly where representatives of the nobility, clergy, and the bourgeoisie from Portugal's different provinces sometimes convened at the demand of the king to assist him in crucial matters. It was similar to the Estates-General in France, an institution where disputes between the different social groups had sparked the French Revolution in 1789. The main demand of the revolutionaries was for the king to return to Portugal and for the Cortes to become the overarching institution, with representatives from all the territories under Portugal's control. The goal was to write a constitution and reform the country according to liberal beliefs, though not all was yet set in place.

Dom João, considering his plan of action after hearing the news from Europe, was in the meantime confronted with a local rebellion in the armed forces that fueled widespread discontent in the urban areas of

Brazil. Finally, though the king feared that returning to Lisbon would end his rule, he was forced to acquiesce to the demands of the rebels, setting sail for Portugal in April 1821 with the royal court accompanying him. He installed his son, Prince Pedro, as the regent of Brazil to rule in his stead.

Meanwhile, the Cortes convened in Portugal to discuss the fate of the kingdom and its overseas territories. During their assemblies over the year, Portuguese members of the Cortes repeatedly denounced any idea of Brazilian self-governance and patronized the Brazilians, whom they saw as subordinates to Portuguese rule. In an interesting turn of events, the representatives ruled in favor of integrating the Brazilian provinces directly under the jurisdiction of Portugal, which essentially degraded Brazil's status back to an overseas colony of Portugal. The representatives also recalled many of the high-ranking Portuguese officers who had remained in Brazil back to Lisbon and demanded the same from Prince Pedro as well.

The pressure mounted on the young prince, as a very prominent liberal Brazilian faction advocated for a break with Portugal. This was also supported by several Portuguese officials residing in Brazil at the time, who organized a petition to convince the prince to disobey the Cortes' orders. Among the main Brazilian liberals was José Bonifácio de Andrada, who would play an important role in the events of the following few years.

Finally, on January 9, 1822, Prince Pedro made his decision to stay in Brazil and defy the demands of the Portuguese revolutionaries. The event became known as the *Dia do Fico*, or "I Shall Stay Day" and marked a significant turning point in Brazilian history. Word soon spread of his pivotal decision. Virtually all of Brazil supported the young prince, though some tried to organize a coup to end Pedro's designs to make Brazil an autonomous state. A quick rebellion was organized by a contingent of Portuguese troops that remained in Brazil, led by officer Jorge Avillez. The rebels quickly found themselves outnumbered. Dom Pedro, instead of punishing the soldiers, offered them the opportunity to set sail for Portugal. Some who swore fealty to the new ruler of Brazil decided to stay and became part of the new army being organized, with José Bonifácio de Andrada as its leader.

Things moved quickly during the next few months. As was usually the case among liberal revolutionaries of the time, different factions emerged that envisioned rather different futures for Brazil before Pedro could consolidate his position and officially declare independence. The conservative wing of Brazilians, including Bonifácio, believed that Brazil should be organized into a constitutional monarchy with an elected government but limited voting rights to certain groups in Brazilian society. More radical liberals preferred universal suffrage, and some even hoped to abolish the monarchy or limit the monarch's powers—though most recognized that the latter scenario was not as likely.

The Portuguese Cortes, upon hearing about the developments that had unfolded in Brazil, sent back word rejecting the actions of the prince and urging him to come back to Lisbon once again. When the news of the Cortes' demands reached Pedro, who was near the Ipiranga River, traveling to São Paulo, he delivered these famous words to his companions: "*Independência ou Morte!*" ("Independence or Death!"). On December 1, 1822, he would be proclaimed the first Emperor of Brazil as Dom Pedro I.

The First Reign

From late 1822 onward, things moved very quickly in the newly independent Empire of Brazil. Dom Pedro I's decision to proclaim independence from Portugal was naturally met with a lot of resistance. Lisbon tried to prepare an adequate response for what it considered treason from the royal prince. Because of stark regional differences and identities, there was no consensus among the different provinces of Brazil. Some, especially in the north, declared their support for Portugal. Nevertheless, the former colonial power could do little to force Brazilians back into subordination. The Portuguese Cortes was in no position to send a large force to South America and could only rely on the pockets of resistance that remained in parts of Brazil to gain control of the colony.

Dom Pedro quickly built a local Brazilian army, and many of his supporters even began organizing local militias to put up a fight against those who resisted. Many slaves were also freed in exchange for their conscription in the army, resulting in the impressive growth of the Brazilian forces by early 1823. What followed was a brief war of independence during which the remaining Portuguese troops in Brazil separately fought against the Brazilian forces loyal to Dom Pedro.

Initially, the Portuguese forces took control of some of the major Brazilian cities, like Salvador and Recife. However, they were quickly forced to surrender, outnumbered by the Brazilians. The Brazilians dominated the Portuguese on the seas, with many Portuguese switching sides and declaring their allegiance to Pedro and his cause. Most

Portuguese forces were defeated or fled by sea by late 1823, and the war was largely over.

What followed was months of stalling from the Portuguese government. Not wanting to give up its hopes of maintaining control over Brazil, it tried to negotiate with local interest groups and international actors. But, by 1824, Dom Pedro had consolidated his position in the newly independent Brazil. Additionally, some foreign powers, most importantly the United States, recognized Brazilian independence, reducing the bargaining chips available for Lisbon. Britain also supported an independent Brazil, seeing it as a viable solution for the protection of its trade interests in South America. Britain did not formally recognize Brazil's independence because they demanded that Brazil end its involvement in the slave trade. However, this was not an immediate option as the country's economy was largely dependent on slave labor.

With the coup of the summer of 1823, Dom João VI regained absolute power in Portugal, further complicating the political situation. Finally, Lisbon agreed to recognize the independence of Brazil after extensive negotiations and mediation from Britain. In August 1825, Brazil agreed to pay a hefty sum of two million British pounds to Portugal as reparations for the economic damages inflicted on Lisbon with the loss of the colony in exchange for recognition. This extremely large amount of capital was simply not available for Dom Pedro at the time, so the emperor's administration was forced to borrow the sum from the British banks. Despite the unfavorable terms, the Brazilian emperor knew that he had to gain recognition from Portugal if he wanted other European nations to formally recognize an independent Brazil and normalize relations.

Domestically, the main political concern for the newly independent Brazil was the question of how it would organize the new government. In May 1823, members of the new constituent assembly first convened to work on the country's constitution and define judicial, legislative, and executive powers and competencies. Extensive negotiations and political maneuvering lasted for about a year until the first constitution was adopted in March 1824.

For its time, it was quite a liberal document and also quite unique. Compared to other Latin American countries that had recently become independent from Spain, Brazil was the only one with a monarchical system. This meant that, initially, there were concerns about the status and role of the emperor and the extent of his powers concerning the parliamentary system the liberal reformers wished to introduce. There were also questions regarding the status of the nobility and other institutions from the *ancien regime*, like the role of the Catholic Church.

Dom Pedro I of Brazil.[6]

The constitution that was eventually adopted and ratified would be kept in place with few modifications until the end of the Brazilian Empire. It was influenced by other similar documents of the time. The 1824 Constitution guaranteed the fundamental individual freedoms of thought and assembly, the equality of all citizens before the law, and religious freedoms (though Roman Catholicism was made the official religion, and other religions could only be practiced privately).

Politically, it instituted a constitutional monarchy where the legislative branch— made up of the Chamber of Deputies and the Senate—was to be elected through indirect and restricted voting. Voting rights were not extended to all of Brazil's population, and certain economic requirements must be met to run for office and be eligible to vote. Only men with an income of at least 100 milreis could vote, but they did not directly choose their candidates. On the other hand, only Catholic males with an annual income of at least 400 milreis could run as a deputy in the lower chamber. Three candidates would be chosen as representatives from each province in the Senate, with the emperor having a final say in who would become a senator—an office that was for life.

The voters voted for an electoral college, which then elected the deputies. Administratively, the province system was mostly kept intact, but the emperor could elect the individual presidents who governed each province. A special Council of State was also introduced, comprised of counselors over forty years old with over 800 milreis of income who served for life and were appointed by the emperor. The role of the Council was to provide advice to the emperor in critical times, though the Council itself had no executive or legislative powers. In addition to the powers mentioned above, the emperor could dissolve the Chamber of Deputies and had a final say on the laws adopted by the parliament, with a right to veto any decision of either body.

Overall, the social and political system of the Empire of Brazil was very distinct from that of other former colonies that had gained independence around the same time, and even from some of the systems put in place in Europe. It was a rather conservative constitutional monarchy, with voting restricted to a clearly defined portion of the population that was economically better off, contributing to more inequality in the empire long term. The emperor had extensive rights and considerable executive powers, able to influence the makeup and functioning of some of the most important institutions.

The first years immediately after independence were marked by a lot of instability and conflict. There was another rebellion in the northern provinces, originating from Pernambuco, that quickly spread over most of northern Brazil in July 1824. The main leader of the insurrection was Frei Caneca (Friar Mug—the clergyman had sold mugs during his childhood), who incited the rebels against the heavily centralized system put in place by the 1824 Constitution. The insurrectionists, mostly made up of wealthy landowners and businessmen of the northeast, announced the formation of an independent state called the Confederation of the Equator, which would include Pernambuco, Paraíba, and Ceará.

The confederation was short-lived, however. The imperial forces subdued the rebels by November, executing the leaders. Though the rebellion was unsuccessful, the strong regional identity of Pernambuco and other northeastern territories of Brazil had manifested once again, and revolutionary sentiments would not immediately die down after 1824.

Another rebellion in the southern part of Brazil eventually forced the new empire into a conflict with the Argentinian United Provinces of the River Plate over the Cisplatina province. Conflict over the control of this land had long characterized Spanish-Portuguese relations, and it would end in a complete military defeat of the Brazilians in August 1828. The Brazilian army was disorganized and weak compared to the Argentinian forces, comprised of forcefully conscripted Brazilians and many foreign mercenaries. Both sides heavily suffered from the conflict that lasted over two years. Finally, a peace treaty was signed thanks to Britain's mediation, and the new independent nation of Uruguay emerged.

These conflicts highlighted some of the issues of the Brazilian economy, which was dealt a heavy blow that resulted in a full-blown financial crisis. The Bank of Brazil, opened in 1808 with the arrival of Dom João VI, was forced to close in 1829, as its gold reserves were completely depleted. Brazilian currency was devalued to fight against inflation but to no avail. Paper money that was issued was largely only valuable in Rio de Janeiro, whereas other major urban centers accepted it at a lower value, causing its value to fall further in relation to international currencies such as the British pound. This, in turn, caused problems with paying civil servants and members of the military, who were becoming increasingly critical of the regime. Anti-emperor liberal sentiments were on the rise in the second half of the 1820s.

The economic crisis was accompanied by a series of events that, when combined with the toll of war, caused widespread social upheaval in Brazil. With the death of Dom João VI of Portugal in 1826, Emperor Pedro was the next in line for the throne. There was serious concern in Brazil that he might bring back the union with Portugal and leave Rio for Lisbon. Dom Pedro, however, abdicated the Portuguese throne in favor of his daughter Maria. Since she was too young at the time to take over, his brother, Miguel, became the king. In the minds of the Brazilians, this decision was very telling. They believed their emperor should have renounced his ties to the Portuguese throne once and for all and established a new dynasty for Brazil. Still, this decision could not have reversed the economic and socio-political troubles experienced by the

Brazilians.

The existing tensions in Brazilian society escalated from 1830 on, once again influenced by the changing situation in Europe, where a liberal revolution in France led to the establishment of the July Monarchy. Liberals all around the world were inspired to push for reforms, especially in such unequal societies in Brazil, where most of the population was excluded from such basic rights as voting in elections.

Brazilian newspapers started publishing prominent liberal manifestoes, and Rio de Janeiro was swept up with calls for the removal of the emperor from office. Adding to the turmoil were demonstrations of support from Portuguese royalists, who supported Emperor Pedro's position. This further angered the liberals, who were in the majority. In March 1831, several prominent military officials sided with the liberals, who demanded reforms. Facing mounting pressure and unable to resolve the situation, Dom Pedro I was forced to abdicate in April 1831 in favor of his son, Pedro II. Unbeknownst to the people of Brazil, this decision would lead to one of the most troubled times in Brazilian history known as the regency period, placing the future of the nation was in uncertain hands.

Chapter Four – From Empire to Republic

The Regency

The regency period was one of the most troubled decades in Brazilian history. In hindsight, it acted as a transitional period from the abdication of Emperor Pedro I in 1831 to the accession of his son, Pedro II (who was just five years old in 1831) in 1840. During this time, Brazil was ruled by a succession of different groups of politicians who tried to maintain order amidst uncertainty and crisis.

Ultimately, the regency period highlighted some of the most entrenched problems of the Brazilian socio-political sphere. Left without the "supervising" force of the emperor, who was an essential part of the still-young Brazilian state, the politicians in power fell victim to an array of conflicting interest groups that left the empire on the brink of collapse. Brazil was faced with serious domestic issues, stemming from the long-standing differences between its social classes and regional identities. Several important rebellions took place, claiming the lives of thousands of people in different parts of the empire as the regents were desperate to uphold their authority in the absence of the emperor.

Most of the measures implemented during the regency were aimed at reforming important aspects of Brazilian society, with the overarching goal of reducing centralized power. In June 1831, the Legislative General Assembly elected three individuals as regents in what is commonly referred to as the triumviral regency. The delegates were chosen to also act as representatives of different regions and interest groups: José de Costa Carvalho, a veteran politician and the founder of one of the most prominent newspapers in São Paulo, *O Farol Paulistano*; João Bráulio Muniz from Maranhão, representing the northern and northeastern regions; and Francisco de Lima e Silva, a military officer from Rio de Janeiro.

The "triumvirate" soon began its work, and one of its chief goals was to limit the extent of the moderating powers of the emperor. The Moderating Power was a special branch of power outlined by the 1824 Constitution that was exclusive to Brazil and vested considerable influence in the hands of the emperor. It was used to refer to the special competencies of the emperor, such as his constitutional right to freely appoint and dismiss ministers, convene the General Assembly or dissolve the Chamber of Deputies, veto proposed legislation, and grant amnesty or pardons to prisoners. Overall, as the name suggests, the emperor was to make decisions of such importance based on his judgment, as he was seen as an individual who stood above the state.

With the Additional Act of 1834, the regency proposed changes to the Constitution that were ultimately adopted by the largely liberal Chamber of Deputies, which had called for more decentralization of power. The Additional Act prohibited the use of the Moderating Power and granted provinces a larger amount of autonomy with the newly implemented regional legislative assemblies, which replaced the preceding General Councils (*Conselhos Gerais*). The assemblies had extensive rights to preside over local judicial and civil affairs without directly involving the central government. They could collect taxes, determine their budgets, and, perhaps most importantly, appoint civil servants in local positions.

The Additional Act also dissolved the Council of State (the exclusive advisory body that could be summoned by the emperor), which the legislators saw as largely useless. Rio de Janeiro was also changed into a Neutral Municipality, becoming an independent federal district, similar to Washington, D.C., in the United States. The influence of American federalism can clearly be seen in other reforms adopted during the regency period, such as the changes applied to the criminal justice code in 1832. These changes amplified the importance of the jury system for many court cases, similar to the American justice system.

Another important reform that preceded the adoption of the Additional Act was the creation of the National Guard—a measure to reform the disorganized Brazilian army, which had just suffered a defeat. Though it still contained many Portuguese-born officers in higher positions, the army's main problems were with ordinary soldiers at the bottom ranks, who had long complained of inadequate pay and poor conditions. The implementation of the National Guard aimed to diminish the importance of the centrally controlled imperial army, where most of the problems existed. Starting in 1831, all twenty-one to sixty-year-old males were required to enlist in regional National Guard regiments that essentially granted the provinces control over better-organized militias. Once enlisted, they were exempt from the imperial army draft. The main goal of the reform, influenced by similar measures adopted in France at the time, was to encourage the local citizens to actively participate in military affairs.

In 1835, elections were held to choose the sole regent who would take over for the triumviral regency that had ruled Brazil since 1831. This had been decided with the Additional Act one year earlier. The consensus since the beginning was that the triumvirate would not last until the accession of Pedro II. Diogo Antônio Feijó, a moderate liberal, became the new regent. Previously, he had served as the minister of justice and had advocated for more authority and decentralization.

During his time as the sole regent, Feijó was opposed by the conservative legislators, many of whom wanted Pedro I to return as the emperor, as well as the "exalted" radical liberal members, many of whom had advocated for the imperium's abolition and the establishment of a federal republic. Feijó was supposed to act as a mediator between the two groups and push moderate liberal reforms that would maintain the status quo of the constitutional monarchy, though he began to experience widespread opposition. More importantly, his tenure as the regent was plagued with provincial instability and the outbreak of two insurrections that would last well beyond the regency period: the Cabanagem in the province of Pará and the "Ragamuffin War" in Rio Grande do Sul in the south. We will cover the nature of these rebellions later, but they significantly weakened the position of Feijó, who faced strict criticism from his rivals for not being able to swiftly pacify the rebels. Eventually, in 1838, he was forced to resign. New elections were held, which were won by the conservative Pedro de Araújo Lima—the last of the regents of the transitory period.

Accession of Pedro II

Even before 1835, the regency had been troubled with several instances of armed uprisings in different parts of Brazil. Though these insurrections had no common agenda, they were all manifestations of strong regional positions against the moderate liberal status quo ushered in by the triumviral regency.

The uprisings were caused by a diverse set of factors. For example, the Cabanada rebellion, which broke out in Pernambuco in 1832, was largely a movement of the rural populations, who had suffered from the economic crisis caused by the decline of sugar and cotton prices. These people, known as the *cabanos*, comprised the lower echelons of northern and northeastern Brazilian society and advocated for the return of Dom Pedro I as the emperor. Though they were pacified in 1835, the *cabanos*, joined with the local Amerindians, slaves, and the mixed population of the region, also revolted in Belem, beginning another uprising known as the Cabanagem that lasted until 1840. Among the immediate causes of this insurrection, which decimated northern Brazil and an estimated fifth of the province's population, was the central government's appointment of a disfavored provincial president.

Salvador also became a center of popular uprisings, one of which was the slave rebellion of 1835 known as the Malê revolt. About 600 Malês, who constituted the Muslim slave minority of the city, rose up and caused chaos in Salvador. Government forces brutally suppressed the slaves in just a day due to the disorganized nature of the uprising, producing mixed responses from the opposing socio-political groups in Brazil. The Malê revolt of 1835 revived a debate about the practice of slavery in Brazil, which would become a prominent topic until the late years of the Brazilian Empire. Several other slave revolts would also break out in cities with large slave populations, such as Rio de Janeiro, though most failed because of the incoherence of the rebels' actions.

Also important was the insurrection known as the Sabinada (1837-1838), named after one of its leaders, Francisco Sabino. The Sabinada gained support from the middle class of Salvador but was eventually suppressed after a siege from the imperial forces that resulted in up to 2,000 casualties. Additionally, inhabitants of the state of Maranhão, who believed that they had been economically disadvantaged by the ongoing financial crisis, rose up in the 1838 revolt of the Balaiada, supported by some urban liberals. They gained control of the city of Caxias and caused widespread destruction for the next three years before being defeated by imperial forces in 1841.

In the southern lands of Rio Grande do Sul, the local *farrapos,* or "the people dressed in rags," revolted in 1835. The longest-lasting of the rebellions of the regency period (until 1845), the Farroupilha Revolt is also referred to as the Ragamuffin War. The leaders of this uprising were mostly wealthy cattle ranchers who had enjoyed close relations with the neighboring Uruguayans since colonial times and protested increased taxes on their province. The rebellion, thanks to great leadership from experienced revolutionaries—like the exiled Italian commander and future leader of Italy's unification, Giuseppe Garibaldi—was a thorn in the side of the Brazilian government. Soon, influenced by its Argentinian and Uruguayan ties, the revolt developed into a separatist movement, with the rebels proclaiming the de-facto independent Riograndense Republic and vigorously defending their position during the regency period.

In short, despite efforts to address some of the issues that had stemmed from the centralization of the Brazilian Empire, the regency experienced widespread problems that put a lot of pressure on the acting government, especially in the second half of the 1830s. Meanwhile, the Brazilian political spectrum was consumed by a firmer divide between liberals and conservatives, which would eventually result in the establishment of the two main political parties in the country.

After the conservative Araujo Lima assumed the position of regent, he proceeded to pass "regressive" measures to further centralize power. Among his regressionist policies was the rolling back of some of the provincial privileges implemented by the Additional Act of 1834. This caused discontent among the liberals but did not change the overall situation for the better. As the tensions continued, political elites began to increasingly favor the accession of the still-too-young Pedro II, who was only fourteen at the time.

The idea of lowering the age for accession to the throne had existed as early as during the first stage of the regency. Despite the liberal-conservative divide, one thing that both sides (except for radical advocates of republicanism) agreed on was the importance of the emperor. The elites knew that the regency was a transitory stage until the young heir to the throne came of age, after which the Brazilian political system would resume as outlined in the 1824 Constitution. The politicians respected the emperor and what the title stood for, largely acknowledging that the monarchy was an indispensable part of Brazil.

Thus, as Brazil's leaders struggled to deal with the ongoing crises, they decided to put their trust in the figure they believed possessed enough authority and respect to lead Brazil back to stability. The option of Pedro I returning as the emperor was no longer on the table, as he had passed away in Portugal in 1834. The next logical option was the young Pedro II.

Interestingly, it was the liberals who presented the legislation that proposed lowering the age of accession to the throne, setting in motion an active campaign to convince the legislators to pass it. Both chambers were eventually convinced. Having gained approval from the parliament, Dom Pedro II ascended to the throne of Brazil in July 1840.

The Second Reign

In hindsight, perhaps no one could have expected the extent of Brazil's transformation during the tenure of Pedro II as emperor, which lasted until 1889 and is referred to as the Second Reign. When he ascended the throne in 1840, the fourteen-year-old Pedro II's empire was experiencing a severe economic crisis, high levels of social inequality, and an ongoing rebellion in the south. Throughout his reign, Brazil emerged as arguably the most powerful nation in South America with a modernized economy and a fundamentally transformed social system. This fifty-nine-year period brought a series of socio-cultural developments that provided the basis of Brazilian life during the twentieth century. Most remarkably, the prominent social and political groups inside Brazil, despite their many differences, got to work to solve the most pressing of Brazil's problems and put the nation on a path toward progress by the end of the century.

The first few years of Pedro II's reign were marked by a continuation of the "regressive" measures initiated by the conservative leaders before his accession, which put considerable power back into the hands of the monarch. The political elites were largely in agreement that strengthening the power of the emperor was the first step toward progress. Many of the emperor's competencies, bestowed on him by the constitutional Moderating Power, were brought back. This was balanced with the implementation of a "reverse" parliamentarian model in 1847, creating the position of President of the Council of Ministers. The emperor would choose the president, who would essentially act as the head of the government. This position was something like the role of a prime minister in most parliamentarian systems. According to the changes, the president of the Council of Ministers would choose the respective ministers. The

Council of Ministers held executive power but needed the trust of both the emperor and the Chamber of Deputies to function.

This was a unique way of dividing the different branches of power in Brazil, with the emperor enjoying a privileged position with his Moderating Power—which made the Brazilian system not fully "parliamentary in the modern sense of the word. Interestingly, this system ensured that the government's makeup was constantly modified and the cabinet was always composed of new ministers. This resulted in more than thirty different iterations of the government until 1889, and representatives from neither political party were excluded. The rapidly changing nature of the Brazilian government made it possible to avoid frequent confrontations about who truly held power. The system felt balanced and was largely unmodified.

These developments in Brazil's political sphere resulted in the entrenchment of a party system that became stable by the 1870s. The old liberal-conservative divide was still prevalent, though the new generation of politicians enjoyed the advantages of a more cohesive political system where both parties developed reasonable agendas and platforms. The emperor played the role of a neutral referee between the two camps, who rightfully considered each other rivals.

The entrenchment of the party system was manifested in the pronounced regional and social support obtained by the two parties by the end of the Second Reign. The conservatives were largely supported by the rich rural landowners and urban merchants from the provinces of Pernambuco and Bahia, the old centers of the Brazilian political and economic sphere. They advocated for the protection of regional economic interests and a strong central government. The liberals, on the other hand, found the main bases of their support in the southern provinces of São Paulo, Minas Gerais, and Rio Grande do Sul.

Important improvements were made to the country's economic structure, including changes to tariffs on imported goods. The Alves Branco Tariff, adopted in 1844, greatly increased customs duties on certain products, some to 30 percent and others as much as 60 percent. Thousands of imported goods were affected, to the dismay of foreign merchants—mostly the British, who largely held a monopoly in the Brazilian markets. The main goal of the policy was to encourage domestic production and local regional centers of manufacturing. Overall, it was a successful move that, paired with other changes aimed at modernization, aimed to make Brazil competitive with the rapidly industrializing Western nations of the nineteenth century.

Meanwhile, a product emerged that defined the socioeconomic situation of late nineteenth-century Brazil: coffee. Introduced to Brazil in the 1720s and first planted in Rio de Janeiro and the surrounding areas in the 1760s, coffee quickly became a pillar of Brazil's export economy. The Paraiba Valley provided an excellent place to grow coffee, becoming a staple of the region despite the difficulties of its harvesting. Dependent on slave labor, the growth of the Brazilian coffee industry coincided with the increasing demand for coffee in European and North American markets. By 1890, coffee made up about 60 percent of Brazil's export economy.

The coffee planters eventually accrued tremendous power in Brazilian society, emerging as the "coffee bourgeoisie" and providing the basis for the later republican developments in the country. The concentration of coffee production in the southern region also resulted in the cementing this part of Brazil as the socioeconomic center of the country. Early after colonization, the northeastern region had been most important because it was where sugar production was the most advanced. With the increased prevalence of coffee as the main product of the Brazilian economy, the southern part of the country once and for all wrestled this title away from the northeast.

The slave question became increasingly prominent during the Second Reign. Slavery in its many different forms had been abolished in the most advanced European societies, which were starting to embrace the principles of classical liberalism. Britain had been a leading force in the end of the Atlantic Slave Trade—a practice started by the Portuguese during colonial times, as you may remember. The British gave themselves the right to inspect any ships in the Atlantic that were suspected of transporting slaves, greatly accelerating the end of the slave trade. By the late 1860s, the last major Western society—the United States—had also abolished slavery.

In contrast to all these developments, the Brazilian economy still largely depended on slavery, with most slaves employed on the coffee plantations of the Paraiba Valley. Rio de Janeiro had a significant number of slaves, as well, with slaves constituting roughly 40 percent of the population.

Thus, the slavery issue was hotly contested among the Brazilians. With coffee becoming a central part of the Brazilian economy, many were against the abolition of slavery, which they believed posed an economic threat. The emperor, on the other hand, had abolitionist tendencies. He had publicly criticized slavery in Brazil on several occasions and was one of the main advocates for gradual reform instead of immediate abolition.

In 1850, a law was adopted by the Chamber of Deputies and passed in the Senate that recognized ships that transported slaves as participants in piracy. This was directly influenced by similar British legislation, the Aberdeen Act, which imprisoned slave traffickers in the Atlantic and tried them in British courts. The adopted measures and more active British involvement resulted in the quick decline and eventual end of the slave trade from Africa into Brazilian ports by the late 1850s.

A logical follow-up to the end of the slave trade would be the abolition of the practice in Brazil for good. Yet again, though everyone (especially the political elite on both flanks) acknowledged that abolition was inevitable, there were disagreements on how to implement it. Most began to agree that a gradual abolition was the way to go. A factor that played a decisive role in the decision was the immigration of large numbers of Europeans to Brazil during the middle of the nineteenth century.

Lawmakers realized that the immigrants arriving in Brazil in increasing numbers could replace the labor of slaves. They began working on policies to guarantee the immigrants did not emerge as an economically dominant class themselves and compete against the landowners, who would be deprived of slave labor. This was in the government's best interests. The rich landowners were, realistically, the backbone of the Brazilian economy. Granted, the way they had gotten rich—by relying on slave labor—was immoral, but something had to be done. International pressure was mounting, and the public was aware of the abolitionist sympathies of the emperor.

The Land Act (Landed Property Act), adopted in 1850 soon after the ban on the slave trade, served exactly this purpose. Its main goal was to legalize the rural properties of the landowners, most of whom had acquired public lands long before through government grants. The law required the landowners to register their estates. Additionally, and more importantly, the law asserted that immigrants could not buy land for three years after coming to Brazil. This was crucial in convincing many of the richest landowners to support abolition. At the least, it provided a foundation for later abolitionist measures.

The government did not want the positive economic trends Brazil had been experiencing for the past few years to stop. It looked to some of the most developed nations for inspiration and noticed a crucial factor that had boosted industrialization in places like Britain and the United States. The obvious and easily implementable answer lay in modernizing the country's infrastructure. Modernity, in the nineteenth century, was associated with railways, which facilitated the inter- and intra-regional transportation of goods, labor, and the military. Thus, rail lines were built throughout the country, linking important centers like Recife with Salvador in the northeast and the inland points of southern coffee production with Rio de Janeiro. Several highways were also constructed to improve the overall transportation system.

Many of the infrastructural projects were made possible thanks to British investments, though a significant number were financed with the revenue accrued by the state through the Alves Branco tariff. Perhaps the most important early industrial businessman in Brazil was Irineu Evangelista de Souza, the Viscount of Mauá, whose investments contributed to the development of the country's infrastructural and financial systems.

With major improvements to modernization and industrialization, the government made a conscious choice to focus on attracting European immigrants as an alternative to slaves. Something that explains this decision was the prejudice of most white Brazilians against African slaves, influenced by the Social Darwinist theories of the nineteenth century that provided a pseudo-scientific justification for European imperialism. If slaves were freed, the landowners would not regard them as equals, and, as was the case, widespread discrimination in their working environments would continue.

Still, in the early 1850s, certain landowners had experimented with an immigrant workforce, such as Senator Nicolau Vergueiro, who first brought Swiss and German immigrant farmers to his coffee plantations. However, the newly arrived Europeans were subject to exploitation and harsh working conditions, which they were not used to in Europe. They soon expressed their discontent and left Vergueiro's estates.

It was not until the 1870s that the government began to actively encourage the immigration of foreign workers. This was because the influx of new slaves from Africa had almost fully stopped and the slaves who remained on the plantations were rapidly aging, affecting coffee production. The government discussed the possible policies with the landowners and passed laws that helped foreigners better integrate into Brazil, for example by subsidizing their passage into the country. São Paulo became the center of European immigration, with more than 10,000 registered immigrants legally moving to the city by 1880.

Many Europeans still found the conditions offered by Brazil to be very difficult to adapt to, spreading unfavorable news of the situation back to their home countries. The Brazilian government combatted this by issuing propaganda pamphlets in European societies like Italy and Germany, which were undergoing massive socio-economic shifts. In these pamphlets, they advertised the opportunities in Brazil in contrast to other major immigrant destinations, such as the United States. Italians were especially targeted, as the country had completed its political unification in the 1870s, accelerating industrialization and switching to a capitalist economy. This had left many of the poorer classes disadvantaged, with more incentives to search for new opportunities overseas.

Thus, in the final decade of the Brazilian Empire, immigration numbers began to drastically increase, reaching their peak during the first decades of the twentieth century. By 1888, São Paulo housed as many as 100,000 immigrants, the vast majority of whom were Italians.

Meanwhile, abolitionists began to rise in prominence in the urban centers of Brazil, founding different groups where they discussed the future of Brazilian society. These groups spread pamphlets and manifestos all around Brazil, convincing much of the population that slavery must be abandoned for good.

With the slave population rapidly shrinking to only about 5 percent of Brazil's population by the late 1880s, the slavery debate was reheated. By then, the immigrant attraction policies had also demonstrated their success. The Brazilian legislators began to work on the issue in the spring of 1888. They were motivated by Princess Isabel, the daughter of Pedro II, who delivered a powerful speech demonstrating the backwardness of slavery and its incompatibility with the modern society Brazil was striving toward. In May 1888, a bill on the abolition of slavery, known as the Golden Law, was drafted and quickly adopted with overwhelming support from both chambers of the National Congress. Brazil thus became the last of the major Latin American colonies to abolish slavery, paving the way for the republican era of the country's history.

In addition to the extensive transformation of the socioeconomic aspects of Brazilian life, one of the main achievements of Pedro II's reign was the reorganization of the military. The National Guard was reformed so that its leaders were chosen by the central government and its appointees in the provinces, and its roles were modified to balance the institution with the imperial army. This measure was adopted in the first half of the 1840s, making it possible for the Brazilian army to gain a significant advantage against the rebels in the south.

As we mentioned, Pedro II had inherited a separatist rebellion in the south, but the imperial government negotiated with the rebels in 1845 instead of continuing the war effort. The self-declared Riograndense Republic was dissolved and rejoined Brazil in exchange for amnesty for the rebels and greater provincial autonomy.

In 1848—the year of liberal revolutions throughout Europe—Brazil experienced the Praieira rebellion in Pernambuco, influenced by the radical republican and socialist ideas of thinkers like Fourier. The rebels caused instability in Recife and the surrounding areas but never accrued enough support to pose a threat to the reorganized Brazilian military. The rebellion was largely pacified soon after it broke out, but pockets of rebel fighters engaged in guerilla tactics until 1850. The Praieira revolt marked the final of the insurrections in Pernambuco, which had historically been prone to such movements. Throughout the reign of Pedro II, no more major revolts broke out in the northeast.

Finally, Pedro II's reign was memorable because of Brazil's successful involvement in a series of conflicts over disputes among the newly independent South American nations. The region had been rather unstable since the beginning of the nineteenth century, and we already mentioned some of the conflicts the Brazilian Empire had to get involved in.

In 1851, the governor of Buenos Aires—Juan Manuel de Rosas—had accrued too much power in Argentina and set his eyes on the ongoing Uruguayan Civil War. Rosas, trying to exploit the chaos and dominate the former territories of the Spanish Viceroyalty of the Rio de la Plata, supported the nationalist Blanco Party. A potential victory for Rosas would greatly endanger Brazil's interests in the region and lead to further destabilization, so Pedro II decided to intervene. Brazil provided support for the Uruguayan liberal Colorado Party and entered the civil war, also gaining support from Argentinian provinces that had been upset with

Rosas' authority. After five months of fighting, Brazil and its allies prevailed, ousting Rosas. The belligerents returned to the status quo, which only increased Brazilian influence in the south.

In August 1864, when Uruguay was plunged into deep political turmoil yet again, Pedro II's representatives presented an ultimatum to the two parties, as the civil war had endangered the safety of Brazilian Natives residing in Uruguay. The Brazilian emperor had demanded a ceasefire and threatened to intervene if denied. Ultimately, the imperial army had to intervene again on behalf of the liberal Colorado Party, though the government at the time never acknowledged official involvement in the war. By February 1865, the Blanco Party was overwhelmed due to the pressure put on its possessions by the Brazilian-Colorado forces, eventually capitulating and ending the conflict. The short conflict was another great political victory for Pedro II's Brazil, as well as for Argentine President Bartolomé Mitre, who had expressed his support for the Colorado Party.

However, the Uruguayan War indirectly led to another conflict—the largest war between states in South American history. Paraguay's nationalist President Francisco Solano Lopez had supported the Blanco faction in Uruguay and was devastated after their defeat at the hands of Brazil. Motivated by imperialist designs, he had denounced Brazil's involvement in the Uruguayan Civil War repeatedly throughout the mid-months of 1864 and had threatened to act. Action materialized in November, as Brazilian forces were still occupied by the war in Uruguay. Paraguayan forces, numbering as many as 80,000 men, crossed into Brazilian territory, forcing Brazil's imperial forces to mobilize against an invasion.

While the initial Paraguayan invasion was repelled, President Lopez also ordered an invasion of Argentine territories that had been disputed between the two countries. This essentially forced Brazil and Argentina into the Treaty of the Triple Alliance with their recent ally Uruguay in May 1865. The combined forces of the alliance proved too difficult for the Paraguayans, who were already struggling by the end of the year. In 1866, the veteran Marquess of Caxias, Lima e Silva from Brazil, assumed command, resulting in a series of victories for the allied forces, who took control of Paraguay's capital, Asuncion, in late 1868. President Lopez fled the city, organizing his forces into guerilla fighting bands. He put up a fight for the next two years before his death during the Battle of Cerro Cora in March 1870.

Above all, the war had a devastating effect on Paraguay. Not only did it lose all its territorial claims, but its population suffered immensely from the conflict. Certain estimates place Paraguayan casualties as high as 200,000, including civilians and soldiers who died from causes associated with the war, like hunger and disease. Brazilian forces remained in Paraguay until 1876, overseeing the creation of a pro-Brazilian government in Asuncion.

Ultimately, because of Brazil's success in these Platine Wars during the 1850s and through the late 1860s, the nation emerged as a dominant force in South America and the Western Hemisphere. Nevertheless, the war brought to the forefront many problems that eventually became troublesome to Pedro II and his government.

The Death of the Empire

The reign of Pedro II ended abruptly in November of 1889, and with it came the dissolution of the Empire of Brazil. It all transpired quickly, with a coup d'état organized by some of the highest-ranking military officers in Brazil forcing the emperor to abdicate. Pedro II obliged without resistance. By the morning of November 16, the Republic of Brazil was proclaimed, with former marshal Deodoro da Fonseca as the interim president of the provisional government until the new political system could be fully adopted.

But what were those behind the coup aiming for? Why had they been dissatisfied with Pedro II's rule?

We already mentioned some of the key areas in which Brazil experienced significant advancements during the long reign of Pedro II. The emperor had struck a comfortable balance between the main political parties of the empire and established a stable system since his accession as a fourteen-year-old. Brazil's economy had grown considerably, and so had its population—reaching about 14,000,000 people by the late 1880s. The nation had made considerable efforts to modernize by improving networks of communication and infrastructure to better connect its vast lands. Geopolitically, Brazil had managed to eclipse virtually all the nations of South America, having emerged victorious from the many conflicts in the south. With an influx of new workers in the form of foreign immigrants, increased urbanization, and normalized relations with European nations, it certainly seemed on the surface that the future of the empire was in safe hands. In fact, since the end of the Paraguayan War, the Brazilian economy had undergone a noticeable shift that favored a new emerging middle class.

However, recent reforms and socio-political developments had left many dissatisfied, not to mention other factors contributing to adverse sentiments against the emperor.

First, those close to the emperor noticed his increasing lack of enthusiasm for fulfilling his duties as emperor. The ailing emperor with poor health was disfavored by the new generation of Brazilian politicians, who had matured during the age of Brazil's progress. The older generation, which had regarded the institute of the emperor as essential to the Brazilian state, were slowly being replaced by new faces that were critical of the emperor and his role.

In addition, Pedro II had lived through the deaths of two of his sons and potential heirs. This had proved especially difficult for the mental state of the emperor, who began to disfavor his daughter, Isabel, as a potential successor to the throne. Although the accession of a woman was not technically impossible, Emperor Pedro believed that only a man could bear a burden as heavy as being the emperor of Brazil. This led to his pessimistic attitudes that could no longer bear the scrutiny of some of his main political rivals.

Pedro II.[7]

Forces in the social and political spheres of Brazil accelerated the decline of Pedro II's regime. One such group was the rich landowners who had largely been left dissatisfied with the abolition of slavery. They had to adapt to the new circumstances and increase their expenditures, even though their revenues were still very high.

The regime had also quarreled with the Catholic Church—one of the pillars of the Brazilian state and the official religion. According to the Constitution, however, the Church operated under the authority of Pedro II, not the pope from the Vatican. This meant that all decisions regarding the organization or operation of Church activities had to go through the emperor before being implemented in Brazil. From the mid-1870s, several prominent bishops had begun to defy imperial authority in hopes of more autonomy.

Similar sentiments had existed in the military, with some of the highest-ranking officers believing that they were undervalued despite their successes in Brazil's many wars. They had long voiced their desire for more autonomy in the army's affairs, which was also strictly controlled by the government. Ordinary soldiers were not getting enough pay or promotions to keep up with the rapidly modernizing economy of the country, feeling unjustly disadvantaged.

Most importantly, however, the main drivers of the coup d'état were members of the republican movement. During the peak of European imperialism, only a handful of powerful nations in the industrialized world had democratic or republican systems—the United States and Great Britain being the chief examples. Brazil had been the only remaining monarchy in Latin America, where the former colonies had all switched to republican systems. Brazilian liberals had long been active in the country's politics, supporting a federalist reorganization of Brazil with more autonomous provinces.

Modernization and urbanization had increased liberal sentiments among members of the public, who began forming societies and clubs where they advocated for the establishment of a Brazilian republic. They saw a monarchic system with this much power and leverage as old-fashioned and pointed at the issue of slavery as a clear indication that it needed to be changed. In the eyes of the republicans, Brazil had been too slow to abolish slavery, and the gradual process had left some of the key groups dissatisfied. Modernity, for them, required an adequate political system where the diverse voices of the public would be justly considered, not one where certain individuals were clearly favored over others.

Brazilian republicans were the leaders behind the drive against the monarchy, and they were joined by other discontent groups by 1889 in voicing their concerns, most importantly the military. This unlikely alliance began to prepare its conspiracy against Pedro II after the adoption of the Golden Law in 1888. To the surprise of many, the rich conservative landowners joined the republican cause against the monarchy, which they believed was biased against them. Though they recouped their losses soon after the abolition of slavery, they were still upset at the emperor and wished to exact their revenge.

The Council of Ministers tried to enact measures during 1889 to please some of the most dissatisfied groups, led by its liberal President Afonso Celso de Assis Figueiredo, the Viscount of Ouro Preto. Among the reforms he had hoped to pass were universal suffrage, a reorganization of the imperial Senate and the National Guard to please the military, and more autonomy for the Brazilian provinces. However, the legislators refused to accept his reforms, further contributing to the anti-regime movements in the nation.

On November 15, 1889, the republican conspirators, joined by hundreds of soldiers and military officers, took to the streets of Rio and organized a swift coup d'état, arresting the Viscount of Ouro Preto (President of the Council of Ministers) and taking control of the government overnight. They were led by Marshal Deodoro de Fonseca, an old commander of the imperial army who had been convinced to join the insurrection days before. Before the coup was staged, the conspirators had spread rumors about a potential crackdown on individuals in the military with republican sentiments, further antagonizing the soldiers against the emperor.

Meanwhile, Pedro II decided to immediately return from his residence in Petropolis, hoping to stabilize the situation. He had believed that the insurrectionists were demanding the replacement of the existing Council of Ministers, and he thought he could pacify them if he elected a new cabinet. Upon his arrival, however, de Fonseca and others informed the emperor that they intended to end the monarchy. However, they stressed that they wanted to avoid a violent clash against forces loyal to the empire. Hearing the news, Pedro II decided not to resist, agreeing to abdicate and go into exile to Europe to avoid further chaos in the country. A new era in the history of Brazil had begun.

Chapter Five – The Struggles of the Brazilian Republic

República Velha

General Deodoro da Fonseca thus became the first president of the newly established republican regime in Brazil, ushering in about forty years commonly referred to as the *República Velha*, or "Old Republic." During these years, Brazil became a constitutional democracy with an elected president, navigating through the first decades of the volatile twentieth century. As is usually the case, the country experienced some of the most pressing challenges during this time, culminating with a revolution that overthrew the government in 1830. In this chapter, we will look at some of the major developments that took place during the First Brazilian Republic.

General Deodoro da Fonseca (1889).⁸

Resistance to the new political situation materialized as early as the first weeks after the proclamation of the republic in November 1889. In the next few days, there were several small-scale uprisings in the military, with monarchist battalions rising up against Fonseca. Rebellions broke out all over the country, including in Rio de Janeiro. The rebels mostly demanded the restoration of the emperor, though their movements were largely disorganized and could not achieve anything of significance.

By late 1890, the new regime had managed to pacify these uprisings, while the politicians in charge of the provisional government began constructing a new order in place of one enforced by Pedro II. Thus came the first republican constitution in February 1891, which officially declared Brazil a constitutional democracy.

Inspired by United States and Swiss federalism, the 1891 Constitution aimed to decentralize power by abolishing the Moderating Power entirely. Firstly, the country was renamed the Republic of the United States of Brazil. The old provinces were renamed "states," and their powers and competencies greatly increased. The National Congress (made up of the Chamber of Deputies and the Senate) was retained, though senators were no longer elected for life; their terms were fixed at nine years.

The executive branch of the government was headed by a president, who served for four years alongside a vice-president, who also acted as the president of the Senate. The two could not be reelected immediately following one term in office. They would be elected through a direct voting system, and voters would be required to provide signatures on their ballots. The old census voting, which had been based on the voters' income, was also abolished, and the voting age was changed to twenty-one. However, women, members of the clergy, soldiers, and the "illiterate and beggars" were excluded from voting.

Finally, the state and the Catholic Church were separated from each other, and the state would be unable to intervene in the affairs of the religious institution.

What did these constitutional changes mean for Brazil? It meant that despite all its claims, the new system was one of the most undemocratic constitutional democracies in the world at the time. The main problems were the restrictive voting conditions and the non-secret voting mechanism, which resulted in a series of essentially rigged elections. In what became known as *coronelismo*, or the rule of the colonels, oligarchs in São Paulo, Minas Gerais, and Rio de Janeiro exercised great influence on the registered voters employed at their plantations, manipulating votes in their favor.

This resulted in the country successively being governed by governments formed by the local Paulista Republican Party (PRP) and the Meneiro (Minas Gerais) Republican Party (PRM). This highlighted the main problem of the republican movement in Brazil: it had not been a widespread popular movement. The elites behind the coup d'état of 1889 could not risk open elections, perhaps believing that the nation's voters would disfavor them.

The pitfalls of the established regime in Brazil began to show one by one. Soon after the adoption of the new constitution, the country was plunged back into an economic crisis. President de Fonseca caused widespread outrage when he wished to dissolve the National Congress to deal with the situation, leading to a naval revolt in Rio de Janeiro organized by one of the admirals of the Brazilian Navy. In November, fearing an escalation that could claim innocent lives, Deodoro de Fonseca resigned. Then-vice president Floriano Peixoto succeeded him in office. Peixoto had himself been an experienced army veteran and was similar minded to his predecessor, hoping to increase both his own powers and the role of the military in the nation's affairs.

The new president presided over some of the most volatile years of the Old Republic, forced to deal with the financial crisis caused by the unregulated development of the Brazilian financial sector since the mid-nineteenth century. His inability to deal with the problems caused by the collapse of the economy, including high levels of inflation, led to the breakout of another naval revolt in March 1893. This time, the revolt escalated into a conflict between forces loyal to the government and rebels. It ended in Peixoto's victory the following year after he had authorized the purchase of foreign warships with state funds.

All this added up to cause another revolt—the Federalist Revolution, which was launched in February 1893. This movement was not ideologically homogenous, consisting of not only radical republicans and advocates of federalism left dissatisfied by the adopted political system but also monarchists who aimed to restore the empire. Some of the rebels were also motivated to rise against the powerful governor of the Rio Grande do Sul—Júlio de Castilhos—who they believed abused his powers. The rebels were finally pacified in 1895 after they joined forces with the naval mutineers, who were also defeated by the government forces. In total, their clashes with the Brazilian army resulted in an estimated 10,000 casualties, further destabilizing the southern part of the nation.

Only in March 1894 were the first presidential elections held in Brazil, resulting in the election of Prudente de Morais—the first president of the country not from a military background. An experienced lawyer and politician, de Morais had served as the governor of São Paulo. He was the first of the succeeding "coffee" presidents from Minas Gerais, which dominated Brazilian politics until 1930.

President Morais further reinforced the concentration of power in the hands of the rich southern elite. Most of them were coffee planters, and coffee exports reached all-time highs in the history of the Brazilian economy. This completed the enduring shift of the socio-political center of Brazil from the north to the south, but it came with severe consequences. Brazil became overly reliant on coffee as its main export, and its agricultural specter almost ignored other plants that could be grown. This meant that Brazil had to import most of its foodstuffs from its neighbors or overseas. Eventually, when the price of coffee decreased in the international market, so did the economic situation of Brazilian coffee planters. The planters lobbied the government to artificially inflate international coffee prices by buying it from the market. This practice began in 1906 and lasted for several years, but soon the government realized that it could not be sustained long-term, and its negative tolls began to show on the Brazilian economy.

Fall of the Old Republic

The domination of Minas Gerais and São Paulo in Brazilian politics resulted in the two regional republican parties constantly winning elections. The parties developed a mutual understanding that gave them a massive comparative political advantage over their northern or northeastern rivals, who could not amass the same resources to contest the elections. This period of southern political supremacy came to be referred to as *café com leite* or "coffee with milk" politics, referring to the two most important industries of the regions—coffee for São Paulo and dairy for Minas Gerais. The nickname also stems from the fact that the two regions cooperated for decades to push their agendas in the domestic political sphere, largely neglecting the problems faced by other regions of Brazil. The socio-economic and political vitality of the south, especially of São Paulo, was thus finally cemented at the expense of the north.

Despite the eventual plunge of coffee prices in the early twentieth century and the disruption of the Brazilian economy, the number of immigrants coming to the country only increased, contributing to the growth of urban centers such as São Paulo. The city soon began to eclipse Rio de Janeiro in almost all respects. By 1910, the city's population had increased to about 400,000 people—a tenfold increase from about 40,000 people in 1885. Santos, a nearby port city, attracted increasing traffic as the main route of export from São Paulo, resulting in its enrichment. In the north, the discovery of rubber in the Amazonas state contributed to the development and urbanization of the region as well, with the city of Manaus becoming a new center.

Rapid urbanization also brought its own problems. For instance, Rio de Janeiro suffered from sanitation and health problems, leading to regular outbreaks of diseases such as smallpox and yellow fever. When officials began implementing changes to the city's urban design and tried to combat the poor health situation in Rio by making vaccination mandatory in the fall of 1904, a large part of the population was outraged. Local soldiers, who had also been dissatisfied with the new republican regime, tried to mobilize the masses into a short rebellion in November known as the Vaccine Revolt, which was promptly suppressed by the government troops.

The pseudo-democratic political system implemented in the 1890s began to show cracks by the second decade of the twentieth century. The decentralized federalist system had resulted in a poorly integrated national economy where there were clear winners and losers. Urbanization, wherever it took place, had transpired without the emergence of a prominent middle class that would take an active part in the socio-political sphere of Brazil. Independent states with their own industries exported their products to foreign markets and largely neglected the domestic market. This contributed to the growth of regional rivalries and further accelerated the development of the more profitable south.

Connectedness between the vast territories of the nation should have been provided by an extensive road and railway network, but this was considered costly and was not favored by potential investors. The lack of advanced communication systems, such as telegraphs in remote areas, meant that it could take a few weeks for information to be transmitted from one place to another. The rich oligarch landowners, who had concentrated most of the nation's wealth in their hands, were not interested in better integrating the different Brazilian provinces to keep their status quo.

The Brazilian economy had also become too dependent on specialized agricultural production and had almost neglected industrialization, outside of certain reforms during the reign of Pedro II. This was partially a legacy of being the last American nation to abolish slavery. Without the prominence of local manufacturing, the country depended on the import of manufactured goods from European and North American markets. This contributed to the lack of technological development in Brazil's industries as well as agriculture, which decreased productivity.

What led to the emergence of social and political movements that eventually ended the oligarchic regime of the Old Republic was World War I. The outbreak of the war in 1914 reshaped the priorities of European nations, most importantly Britain, slowing the export of its manufactured goods to foreign markets.

The war, the deadliest in human history up to that time, not only put great pressure on the economies of the belligerents but also indirectly affected the situation elsewhere. Brazil experienced another severe crisis and inflation caused by the drop in coffee's demand and prices around the world and the government's efforts to subsidize local producers.

With coffee production plummeting, those who had worked for the planters began to join the urban middle and working classes, resulting in a surprising increase in the domestic production of manufactured goods. Brazilian factories produced goods that were cheaper in the domestic market, and the domestic flow of capital began to finally increase as the coffee oligarchs struggled to maintain their domination. The disruption of the import of foodstuffs also created a demand for the diversification of Brazilian agriculture, though coffee and sugar were never ousted as the primary export goods.

With the influx of foreign immigrants from Europe during and after the war years, prominent political ideologies of the time—most importantly anarchism and socialism—were on the rise. Widespread dissatisfaction with the country's socio-economic and political situation was increasingly voiced. People began to realize that the status quo favored only a handful of individuals, while the great potential of the country was not being utilized by the government, which was dominated by the interests of the oligarchs.

The emerging urban middle class formed a loose alliance with factory workers, industrialists, and people employed in the public sector, advocating for reforms after the First World War. Their demands ranged from the implementation of universal suffrage to a reformation of the educational system, the industrialization of the nation, and the improvement of workers' conditions.

Anti-government sentiments were shared by some of the army officers and, together, these groups formed a coalition for the 1922 presidential elections. Despite their best efforts, they lost, and the PRM retained the oligarchic status quo. The disappointing result became the subject of a protest in Rio, where some members of the military launched an unsuccessful rebellion.

This began an eight-year struggle between the government and its southern oligarchic supporters and dissidents who criticized the regime, led by junior military officers—the *tenentes*. The *tenentes* did not give up their hopes of forcing the government to pass national reforms that would consider the interests of most of the population. Over the next few years, they were a thorn in the government's side, organizing minor rebellions all over the country. Their efforts of resistance increased nationalist sentiments among the public, which began to increasingly mobilize against the government.

The Vargas Era

On October 29, 1929, with the United States stock market crash, Brazil was plunged into the Great Depression. Coffee prices plummeted once again on the international market as different nations tried to combat the inflation and unemployment caused by the financial crisis. Brazil's government, as before, tried to artificially manipulate coffee prices to guarantee a reliable stream of income for the coffee planters, who had become more and more dependent on the interventionist policies of favorable politicians. However, as is usually the case in an economic crisis, the middle and lower classes were hit the hardest, adding to their discontent and pushing the tensions to new highs ahead of the 1930 presidential elections.

A heterogeneous alliance of the middle and working classes, *tenentes*, industrialists, and socialists was formed in 1929. It nominated Getúlio Vargas as its representative against the Paulista nominee Julio Prestes for the 1930 elections.

Vargas had himself come from a family of landowners from Rio Grande do Sul, earning his name among the political actors of the 1920s. He recognized the fundamental problems Brazil faced, and his platform included promises about industrialization, nationalization of the country's resources, the extension of voting rights, and reformation of the federalist system.

Throughout the years, he had accrued enough political clout from the dissatisfied groups within the country to emerge as essentially a populist leader, claiming that the "real people" had been disadvantaged by a group of corrupt elites—something that resonated deeply with the public.

For the 1930 elections, he had strategically chosen João Pessoa from the northeastern Paraiba region as his running mate, exploiting the long regional rivalry of Brazil. As he campaigned extensively before the elections, hopes were high that the political dominance of the southern coffee elite would once and for all be put to an end.

Getulio Vargas.⁹

The 1930 election, like most of the prior elections in Brazil, was plagued with widespread corruption and fraud, ending in the victory of Julio Prestes with 57 percent of the votes. Vargas had only been victorious in Rio Grande do Sul (with over 99 percent of the votes), Minas Gerais, and Paraiba, accruing a total of over 700,000 votes. He and his coalition refused to accept the results of the election, contributing to the rising tensions inside the country.

Crucially, in June of 1930, Joao Pessoa was murdered in Recife, sparking widespread protests and instability in the northeast that had to be dealt with by government forces. Vargas, having built an extensive network of contacts in the military sympathetic to his platform, began planning a conspiracy to seize power. The conspirators devised detailed plans to take over several of the country's most important locations, beginning their actions in early October of the same year before Prestes could enter office and begin his duties.

Revolutionary forces acted quickly and decisively, gaining the upper hand by the middle of the month, with Vargas publicly demonstrating his intentions. By October 24, President Washington Luis had been ousted, and a military junta was established in Rio to oversee the ceding of power. With the revolution of 1830, the Old Republic came to an end and the Vargas era began.

Starting in November 1930, Getúlio Vargas exercised full control over the political affairs of Brazil. The very first decisions taken by him and his supporters were aimed at depriving his political rivals of influence and centralizing power in the hands of the president. The obvious issue with Vargas and the broad alliance that had supported his ascent to power had been the lack of a cohesive program, something that was necessary if the new president wished to drag the country out of the recession caused by the Great Depression. Partly to give himself time to consolidate his position, Vargas repealed the 1891 Constitution, dissolved the main legislative bodies of the country, and assumed the leadership of a "provisional government" before a new constitution was enacted in 1934.

To address the country's dire economic circumstances, Vargas adopted a series of interventionist policies that granted tax breaks to certain groups, imposed import quotas on foreign goods, and encouraged the expansion of the domestic industrial sector. These policies, again, did not follow a sound economic or ideological agenda. Instead, they were mainly immediate efforts at consolidating support from the rising middle classes.

Importantly, Vargas linked his state interventionist policies and the necessity to industrialize with nationalism, publicly criticizing the influence of foreign actors on Brazil. The main interest group Vargas favored were the northeastern landowners, who had been a significant force in the coalition behind the new president. To repay for their support and take a jab at the influence of the southern coffee oligarchs, Vargas promoted the diversification of the country's agriculture in the northeast, reasserting their leverage on the workforce. This went against some of the more socialist promises of Vargas' platform. Rural workers became more disadvantaged, fueling the rise of leftist sentiments against the new ruler.

It thus became apparent early on that Vargas would continue to favor his supporters with his socio-economic measures and increase his political power through centralization. This led to several revolts against the new regime, most of which were promptly suppressed by local loyalist troops. The army under Vargas was also not afraid to use force against a wave of left-wing and student protests. In the summer of 1932, the dissatisfied southern coffee oligarchs launched the Constitutionalist Revolution to try and oust Vargas from power, resulting in up to 5,000 casualties. The revolt was sparked after government forces had killed four student activists in May, but the rebels could not amass enough support to seriously challenge Vargas' regime.

The attempted revolution made Vargas realize he could not move further toward his goals of centralization without catering to the coffee planters. For this reason, he began to increasingly appeal to their interests, pardoning their debts and placing favored officials in positions of power in São Paulo and Minas Gerais. He increasingly expressed nationalist anti-leftist sentiments, forgetting that he had essentially come to power through a platform to end the dominance of the landowner elites.

The ambiguity of his stances and the lack of cohesion that usually characterizes the actions of populist leaders manifested itself in the 1934 Constitution, adopted after extensive work by the National Constituent Assembly. The biggest political changes included the implementation of secret ballot voting and the extension of suffrage to women. It also granted extensive rights to the government to regulate the economy. Brazilian resources were nationalized, and a corporatist system was set up, promoting cooperation between the largest interest groups inside the country (not only business corporations).

Vargas' regime was showing great resemblance to some of the ultra-nationalist and fascist regimes gaining prominence in contemporary Europe, namely those of Benito Mussolini in Italy and Adolf Hitler in Germany. Vargas began to adopt increasingly fascist rhetoric after the Communist uprising of November 1935 in Recife and Rio, which was quickly suppressed by government forces. The president began to blame the leftist groups for their continued efforts to destabilize the Brazilian state. The uprising had essentially provided Vargas with a new scapegoat.

Knowing that he would be barred from re-election in 1938, he addressed the nation in November 1937 with a radio speech, informing the country of a Communist plot to overthrow the government. According to him, radical leftist groups had devised the "Cohen Plan" with which they wanted to establish a Communist dictatorship in the country. However, no such conspiracy existed. The president had made it up to justify some of the measures he would take next, seemingly to defend the country from the revolutionaries. Thus, following his speech, Vargas proceeded to declare a state of emergency and dissolve the Congress. He quickly announced a new constitution that granted the president virtually unlimited powers and contained anti-communist, nationalist rhetoric.

So began a new era in the history of Brazil deemed *Estado Novo*, or the "New State," also referred to as the Third Brazilian Republic. For the next eight years, Vargas essentially acted as the dictator of the country, justifying his stay in power by scapegoating leftist groups and cracking down on whoever dared to express their opposition. Brazil was turned into a police state, with the army Vargas' main ally in maintaining the regime.

Political and civil society opponents, critics of the regime, suspected dissenters, and activists were imprisoned and tried in tribunals set up by the regime to pursue its own ends. All political parties were dissolved by a presidential decree, including the fascist Integralist Party, which had until that point been the main political ally of Vargas against the Communists. Censorship laws were put in place and enforced by the regime. Economic measures were taken to push industrialization and quell any discontented sentiments the public might have against the dictator. State companies were created to better control Brazilian resources.

With the outbreak of World War II, Vargas proceeded to justify his further stay in power based on the tense international situation. Brazil was formally neutral at first, though Vargas' efforts at forming close ties with the United States meant that the country provided valuable wartime materials to the Allies, such as rubber and iron. The rubber industry, based around the Amazon basin, was especially developed, as the Axis powers had taken over the largest rubber reserves in Southeast Asia.

Only in 1942, after its merchant ships were sunk by German submarines, did Brazil join the war on the side of the Allies. The Brazilian Expeditionary Force was sent to Europe, achieving great prestige for the Brazilians despite its lack of training and adequate equipment compared to other Allied nations. In turn, the United States granted Brazil land-lease grants and air support throughout the war, which helped Vargas sustain his position until 1945.

The Fourth Brazilian Republic

Ironically, the success of the Brazilian Expeditionary Force (BEF) was one of the factors in the decline of Vargas' authority by the end of 1945. With international tensions dying down and the war ending, pressure against Vargas from inside the country began to increase. Returning BEF soldiers were put under surveillance by the government, which feared they might emerge as leaders of a popular movement against Vargas.

These fears materialized in another non-violent military coup in late October 1945, which succeeded in deposing Vargas and ending the Estado Novo. Led by several army officers, the coup followed the fixing of the presidential elections on December 2 of the same year. Crucially, Vargas had announced plans to draw up a new constitution and had declared his intent to run. In fact, this might have been the reason he wished to change the constitution, as the previous iterations did not allow for the acting president to run immediately for a second term. With pressure from the public mounting and many feeling threatened by the idea that Vargas could stay in power, the coup d'état of October 29 was organized. Vargas was forced to resign, though the former dictator remained active in Brazilian politics.

In the elections held in December of the same year, Eurico Dutra, the Minister of War during Vargas' regime, emerged victorious with about 55 percent of the popular vote. He was from the same center-right Social Democratic Party founded by Vargas (the other being the Brazilian Labor Party) and had defeated the candidates from the conservative National Democratic Union and the Brazilian Communist Party.

A new constitution was established the very next year, marking the return of the country to democratic rule and the beginning of the Fourth Brazilian Republic. The constitution repealed the authoritarian measures of 1937 and aimed to restrict the powers of the president to avoid the rise of another Vargas. Presidential terms were fixed at five years instead of four, and greater autonomy was granted to the Brazilian states. All in all, the presidency of Eurico Dutra marked a relatively peaceful and stable five years. During this time, the government forged closer relations with the United States and modestly invested in key sectors of the Brazilian economy.

Interestingly, despite his deposition, Getúlio Vargas still maintained a high level of popularity among a certain base of supporters. He managed to become a senator by amassing popular support from Rio Grande do Sul and São Paulo and served during the presidency of Dutra. Even more importantly, the 1950 elections would mark Vargas' return as a presidential candidate from his populist Brazilian Labor Party and, ultimately, his victory in the elections with 48 percent of the national vote.

Vargas was inaugurated for his second term in January 1951, and his return as the president marked one of the most perplexing periods during the Fourth Republic. Vargas had technically defeated his opponents during the elections, though the number of votes he and his party had received was not enough to put him back in the position he had enjoyed in the 1930s. The party did not hold a majority in the National Congress, and the reduced powers of the president outlined in the new constitution meant that Vargas did not have free reign over the policies adopted during his second term. Still, the president-elect relied on populist rhetoric to stir up nationalist sentiments in the Brazilian public and succeeded in reinstating some of his old political allies to positions of power.

The Brazilian economy was still struggling to keep up with modernization, and the government was torn between adopting a neoliberal or interventionist stance. Some of the measures taken during Vargas' second presidency included doubling the minimum wage—a radical policy that only contributed to the rising inflation. Government spending was still too high, resulting in budget deficits and an increase in the national debt. Perhaps the most important decision of the government was the creation of a national petroleum company, Petrobras, to better develop the country's oil reserves.

Meanwhile, Vargas' main opponents continued to voice their concerns over his return as the president. This time, thanks to the existence of a free press and freedom of expression—two things not available to the critics during Vargas' dictatorship—their disapproval of the government reached new highs. Members of Vargas' administration were increasingly criticized, and some were dismissed from office by 1954.

The main anti-Vargas opposition party—the National Democratic Union—was joined by some members of the military in its critical remarks against the president. This created the sense that another conspiracy was brewing, putting further pressure on Vargas.

In early August 1954, there was an attempted murder of an opposition journalist and a vocal critic of Vargas, Carlos Lacerda. Lacerda had begun a campaign to run for the Chamber of Deputies and was frequently threatened, forcing him to hire a group of bodyguards. Ultimately, he survived the attack, but one of his bodyguards (a former air force officer) was killed, and another was wounded. The news of the attempted assassination soon hit national headlines, and after an investigation, one of Vargas' personal guards, Gregório Fortunado, was identified as the man who had ordered the assassination.

This set off another wave of public protests against Vargas and his administration, which was accused of widespread corruption. The public was joined by members of the military, who expressed their wish for Vargas' resignation. Following the scandal, President Vargas committed suicide in the presidential palace on August 24, fearing that a military coup against him was imminent. He left behind a letter in which he claimed that he had done everything for Brazil.

After an interim period during which three different individuals were chosen to fulfill the duties of the president, the former Governor of Minas Gerais, Juscelino Kubitschek de Oliveira, clinched a victory in the presidential elections held in October 1955. His ascendency marked the beginning of the end of the Fourth Brazilian Republic, which lasted until 1964.

Kubitschek, who became president with just over one-third of the total votes, was one of the most ambitious figures in the history of twentieth-century Brazil. His "Fifty Years in Five" program was an extensive plan to push for reforms in a wide range of social, economic, and political aspects of Brazilian life. This included proposed changes to such important fields as the country's infrastructure, communication and transport systems, energy sector, and education. In short, he wanted to rapidly industrialize the country, and his policies were a testament to his intentions. The government took over and began investing in industries such as hydroelectric power production and iron and coal mining and expanded its control over the petroleum industry.

Perhaps the most evident legacy of Kubitschek's administration was the construction of a new capital city—Brasilia—which was designed by prominent Brazilian architect Oscar Niemeyer. Strategically constructed nearly 600 miles west of Rio de

Official presidential portrait of Joscelino Kubitschek.[10]

Janeiro in an underdeveloped part of the country, Brasilia was supposed to attract a large number of inhabitants and accelerate the growth of the region.

Kubitschek's administration and decisions were heavily criticized, however. This was mainly because the state greatly increased its expenditures and added to its national debt by borrowing from foreign sources. By the end of his term, Brazil's debt had increased to 300 million USD, more than a threefold increase from 1956. Much like his predecessors, the president was criticized for neglecting the welfare of the lower strata of Brazilian society in favor of his goals to accelerate economic growth. Though the influx of foreign capital did result in the growth of several national industries, it has also increased domestic wealth inequality. Living standards remained horrible for many Brazilians in the rural areas as well as in the urban centers. This resulted in Kubitschek's support plummeting by the end of his tenure as president, and he was replaced after the 1960 elections by Jânio Quadros, a candidate from Vargas' old National Labor Party.

An extremely popular candidate at the time of his election, Quadros assumed the office of the president in 1961 and emerged as a vocal critic of the measures undertaken during the previous administration. He adopted the image of a politician with a desire to root out the widespread corruption in Brazilian politics but was unable to implement effective policies to address the problems faced by Brazil. This is why Quadros' presidency was marked by a subtle return of populism.

For instance, the president proceeded to ban gambling in the country, justifying his decision by saying that it was one of the main causes of inflation. The president also adopted a controversial foreign policy initiative by reestablishing diplomatic relations with the socialist and Communist nation of Cuba, seemingly to make Brazil a neutral nation during the Cold War.

We must remember that the United States had been Brazil's closest international ally before these developments, with intentions to deepen the relationship expressed early on by both sides. It was during Quadros' tenure as president that this relationship took a first hit. With it came a dissatisfied National Congress. Quadros lost his support and eventually resigned in August 1961, just five months after taking office.

Chapter Six – The Birth of Modern Brazil

The Coup of 1964

Jânio Quadros' resignation was an unexpected decision. Many have identified it as a move the president had hoped would cause the public to demonstrate its support toward him and make him return to power. No such support materialized, however. Instead, the National Congress recalled Vice President João Goulart from his trip to China to assume the office. (The vice president's mission was to normalize relations with the Communist nation, per Quadros' policy.)

Certain prominent individuals, however—mostly military officers—were against Goulart, believing he was himself a Communist and therefore an enemy of Brazil. The military ministers of the navy, army, and the air force vetoed Goulart's accession and wanted to hold new elections. Still, their decision did not amass widespread public support, and the Congress launched the Legality Campaign to ensure that Goulart became president.

Led by several state governors, military officers, and constitutionalist legislators, the campaigners believed that the ministers' decision to veto Goulart violated the constitution. Members of the public and parts of the army were mobilized, but, fortunately, no armed confrontation took place between the two groups.

Instead, they reached a compromise. Goulart was sworn in as a temporary replacement for Quadros but with limited powers that were implemented after changes were made to the constitution. Instead of the president, the prime minister assumed executive powers. This system lasted until early January of 1963 when voters took to the polls in a national referendum and voted in favor of reversing the amendments made to the constitution. This meant the parliamentarian system was abandoned, amendments were repealed, and pre-1961 powers were returned to President Goulart.

Nevertheless, it was obvious by this time that the political tensions in the country had not faded away. Quadros' resignation had caused massive polarization between the different groups in Brazil. Throughout the early 1960s, strikes and mass protests were common in the largest Brazilian cities, but little was done to address the problems faced by many Brazilians.

Once his powers were increased, Goulart tried to push for left-leaning reforms, such as more active involvement of the state in the nation's economy and land redistribution. In theory, these reforms would have diminished the power of some of the wealthiest landowners who still dominated the Brazilian social and political sphere. The president's critics increasingly thought of him as a Communist, and his support in the National Congress began to wane.

Amidst the international crises that were caused by the Cold War, such measures also drew the interest of the United States, which saw itself as the main enemy of the spread of Communism around the world. American-Brazilian relations continued to deteriorate as President Goulart refused to stop implementing his measures. Meanwhile, anti-Goulart movements began to gain prominence, and the instability and polarization that existed inside the country resulted in another conspiracy against the president, supported by the United States.

So was launched the military coup d'état of March 31, 1964, which succeeded in deposing Goulart. The uprising began after prominent members of the military joined anti-Goulart protests that had broken out in Minas Gerais. Among the chief leaders were Humberto Castelo Branco, who ultimately became the new president after Goulart was overthrown. Members of the National Congress also supported the insurrection, having secretly communicated with the US State Department for support against the seemingly Communist Goulart.

With "Operation Brother Sam," the US Air Force and US Navy had been mobilized to transport supplies to the coup's instigators and were ready to arrive in Brazil. However, their involvement in the coup was not necessary, as pro-Goulart groups could not to provide resistance to the coup. Rebel troops proceeded to occupy key positions in Rio de Janeiro and São Paulo, convincing more and more soldiers to join their cause. Goulart fled into exile to Uruguay the very same day, and by April 2, he was no longer able to mount resistance.

Dictatorship in Brazil

The new regime was maintained in Brazil for the next twenty-one years, marking a transformative period for the country amidst a turbulent international climate. The instigators of the coup instantly began implementing measures aimed at strengthening and legitimizing the new regime. Instead of repealing the 1946 Constitution, the military government adopted extra-legal decrees, the Institutional Acts. These acts gave the leaders of the coup political leverage and the self-ascribed authority to act beyond the borders of the constitution. The first of such acts was issued on April 9, 1964, greatly increasing the powers of the president. Two days later, the National Congress elected General Castelo Branco to serve as president for the remainder of the term of former President Goulart.

Castelo Branco's tenure as president kicked off relatively calmly. The first dictatorial measures he took came only in October 1965 with the adoption of the Second Institutional Act. With this decree, the executive was once again granted virtually unlimited powers, while those of the judiciary and the legislative branches were greatly reduced. The president could essentially choose favored lawmakers and governors, as well as dismiss them from office if he saw fit. Deputies critical of the regime, as well as left-leaning members of the National Congress, were thus purged, and many former military officers were given ministerial positions. Castelo Branco and his government then proceeded to outlaw all but two political parties: the National Renewal Alliance (ARENA)—a far-right party backed by the ruling government—and the Brazilian Democratic Movement, which constituted the "centrist" opposition.

A new constitution was also written in 1967, reaffirming the supremacy of the president and the Brazilian Armed Forces as his right-hand institution. The president could propose legislation to the National Congress, which had thirty days to review it. If there was no clear response from the Congress during the thirty days, the proposed decrees would automatically become laws. State autonomies were reduced, and fundamental freedoms of assembly, for example, were restricted. The competencies of the police were also increased; those suspected of being criminals could be freely imprisoned and tried in courts. Another important change impacted the election of the president and state governors. The elections were made indirect: the National Congress chose the president, and state legislatures chose their governors. In actuality, these measures only gave more power to the government to perpetuate the regime and increase its powers. The country's name was also changed to the Federative Republic of Brazil.

Castelo Branco was replaced as president by one of the toughest anti-communist hard-liners of the military dictatorship, Artur da Costa e Silva. His time in office was marked by the adoption of more authoritarian and nationalist measures that were often the subject of public protest.

The government proceeded to censor the Brazilian media, which had emerged as one of the most vocal critics of the regime despite supporting the deposition of Goulart in prior years. Special state bodies were created to oversee the implementation and enforcement of censorship laws, acting under the Ministry of Justice. Virtually all fields of media and communications, including radio, television, newspaper, and cultural spheres like theater or music, were censored by the government starting in 1968, leading to the creation of a "black market" for information transmission. These changes were made possible through several Institutional Acts. During this time, these decrees became a staple mechanism for increasing the power of the military dictatorship and overcoming the barriers created by the constitution.

It was also during this time that the systematic use of violence became another staple of the military dictatorship. The government essentially gave the police free reign to crack down on non-sympathetic members of the public. The state had engaged in similar activities during Vargas' presidency, but this time the scope of police brutality reached new highs, and the methods of torture were especially brutal. Those suspected of being members of secret left-wing organizations or protest movement organizers were imprisoned and tortured. This was especially the case during the first few years of the military dictatorship when protests by students, left-wing groups, artists, and civil society members were more common. Clashes with the riot police would result in hundreds of deaths and injuries and even more imprisonments.

To make them more effective, Brazilian police and members of the army were specially trained by US and UK intelligence experts who specialized in torture methods. The troubled legacy of the human rights abuses during the Silva regime lives on in Brazil, and many efforts have been made since the 1980s to root out the systematic brutal practices of the dictatorship.

Silva's presidency was cut short in August 1969 when he suffered a cerebral thrombosis that incapacitated him. Instead of Vice President Pedro Aleixo taking over, however, a military junta comprised of three generals assumed control of the country and decreed several Institutional Acts to legitimize itself.

The leaders of the junta justified their decision by the fact that the National Congress was still in recess. They wished to proceed by sharing the duties of the president among the three, but this proved impossible due to protests from the political and public spheres. Thus, a new election date was set in late October. Of course, a National Renewal Alliance candidate—Emílio Garrastazu Médici—prevailed, becoming the next president of the country in late 1969.

The repressive measures of Silva's presidency were taken to new highs during Médici's tenure as the government continued to exercise extensive control over public life. In general, the regime continued to crack down on political dissidents and vocal critics of the government. It restricted individual freedoms, censored the press, and adopted an increasingly nationalist and anti-leftist rhetoric.

However, the oppressiveness of Médici's term was complemented by great efforts to boost the nation's economy, which resulted in the "Brazilian Miracle," to the surprise of many domestic and international observers. Government policies resulted in the magnificent average annual growth of 11.2 percent of the country's GDP, and inflation rates were kept stable until late 1973. Thanks to the plan devised by a group of technocrat economists led by Antônio Delfim Netto, Brazil managed to attract foreign investors and boost domestic production in industries such as car manufacturing. The output of the national economy was diversified, and coffee was no longer the main export of the country, with its share dropping to about 15 percent in the first half of the 1970s.

The Brazilian Miracle had been partially due to the favorable international financial situation, which made it easier for Brazil to borrow money from overseas sources. Though the country's total GDP increased, there were also clear winners and losers of the economic policies, which favored the accumulation of capital in the hands of the wealthiest members of society. The state proceeded to drop many of its social welfare programs, which hit the lower social strata the worst. Additionally, the oil crisis of 1973 dealt a massive blow to the Brazilian economy, as petroleum had been among the most imported resources for the country.

By the end of Médici's term, the socio-economic situation in Brazil was very contradictory. The country was on an upward industrialization course with one of the worst qualities of life for the large majority of its society.

Abertura

The election of Ernesto Beckmann Geisel as president in 1974 is usually associated in Brazilian history with the beginning of liberalization and the gradual transition away from a fully authoritarian dictatorship. This time has become known as the period of "political opening" or *abertura*, but it is not to be confused with the era of radical changes that brought about the instant re-democratization of Brazil. In fact, Geisel was elected according to the established "tradition" of the military regime since 1964—nominated by the leadership of the armed forces and elected without any real opposition. He had been chosen because of his army credentials, close connections to the regime since the time of Castelo Branco, and the influence of his brother, who was the Minister of War. Nobody foresaw at the time that his tenure would begin a gradual process of liberalization that would continue for the next ten years.

His moderate leanings were well-known inside ARENA, and to be sure, there was some opposition against him from the most ardent supporters of the dictatorial regime. However, it is not easy to pinpoint the reasons behind the gradual liberalization program he adopted during his presidency.

One of the main reasons might have been the crisis Brazil had found itself in since 1973, caused by the fluctuation of international oil prices. The roots of this problem could be traced back to the strict military hierarchy imposed. Geisel thought that it would be better for Brazil in the long term to slowly separate the military from governmental affairs. Although this could not be done instantly for obvious reasons, his administration ultimately was responsible for at least creating an atmosphere that allowed the opposition to voice its concerns.

Yet, many of the measures of the *abertura* were followed by equally conservative and authoritarian crackdowns, some reminiscent of Médici's rule. For instance, opposition parties were allowed to use radio and television during their campaigns for the state legislature elections that were held in November 1974. The Brazilian Democratic Movement (MDB) was thus able to finally gain more representation in regional legislatures. However, this was followed by a crackdown on the Communist Party and press censorship measures of 1975, which were in keeping with the strong anti-communist stance of the military regime.

In short, what Geisel correctly recognized was the fact that Brazil's political system was not sustainable and changes could only be imposed from positions of power. The 1974 state legislature elections went a long way to revitalize the opposition movement, and subsequent elections were all held in a similarly free manner. This resulted in the MDB winning even more seats in the National Congress in 1976. For the first time, this may have threatened the position of ARENA. Geisel was thus quick to utilize the powers granted to him by the Fifth Institutional Act to dissolve the Congress in 1977 and create structures that guaranteed the accession of his desired successor. This approach of allowing for gradual democratizing advances and then countering them with authoritarian measures became a staple of his presidency.

Ultimately, Geisel's approach gave many people who had been disenchanted with Brazilian leadership a sense of hope and the desire to take to the streets. Thus came the labor strike movements of the greater São Paulo area in 1978, the first organized strikes after the repressive policies of the government. Organized by the left-wing parties and led by then-activist and eventual president Luiz Inácio Lula da Silva, workers began to demand wage increases and better conditions. Up to half a million people took to the streets, and the government ultimately acquiesced to their demands.

All these developments added up. By the end of his term, President Geisel had effectively ended press censorship, repealed the Institutional Acts that granted the president virtually limitless powers, and revived the political opposition.

Geisel's presidency also saw significant shifts in the direction of Brazilian economic and foreign policy. Though the president continued to borrow heavily to deal with the trade deficit and inflation, many of his measures were directed at making Brazil less dependent on imports in the long term. The government renewed heavy investments into the state's infrastructural and communication projects, including in rural and underdeveloped areas that had previously been neglected. Notably, he supported the diversification of the Brazilian energy sector and the country's dependence on oil imports by encouraging the development of the ethanol production industry.

The technocratic group of economists responsible for the neoliberal policies during the Brazilian Miracle was dismissed, and the country adopted a foreign policy that complemented the economic changes. For instance, though the United States remained a strong trade partner, Brazil began to forge closer ties with European and Asian nations. Geisel managed to strike a deal with West Germany worth roughly ten billion USD, financing the construction of eight nuclear reactors in the country, following his intention to diversify the energy sector.

Nuclear power was a sustainable and, in the long-term, cheap solution to Brazil's dependence on oil. Brazil's new international partners and reduced reliance on the United States alarmed Washington, which responded by increasing its criticism of the Brazilian regime's continued human rights violations. Ultimately, this put more pressure on Geisel and his successor, João Figueiredo, to tone down the government's repressive measures against political dissidents and opponents.

Democratization

João Figueiredo, who assumed the office of president in March 1979, continued the political liberalization begun by Geisel. Interestingly, Figueiredo had been a long-standing member of the military regime, even serving as the head of the National Intelligence Bureau and overseeing many of the violent practices of the regime during the 1970s.

Figueiredo was sworn in while Brazil was experiencing yet another economic crisis caused by the instability of the global market, with inflation reaching as high as 110 percent in 1980. The crisis hit the lowest sectors of Brazilian society the hardest, who continued to organize mass demonstrations against the government. The government could not deal with these domestic problems and had to ask the International Monetary Fund for a bailout in 1983. After rigorous negotiations, the IMF loaned Brazil a huge sum of money at a high interest rate. But the IMF was upset when Figueiredo's administration did not reduce spending to uphold its part of the deal. Though the country's GDP technically continued to grow during his presidency, so did inflation, which had doubled to about 223 percent by 1984.

One of the most important policies of Figueiredo's administration—one that perhaps played the biggest part in re-democratizing the country—was the amnesty law for political exiles and dissidents who had been previously persecuted by the military government. The amnesty law was adopted despite harsh criticism from several prominent hard-liner army officials, who wished to maintain the status quo. Occupying important positions in the government, they perhaps feared they would be punished for their crimes if they gave up power. Importantly, in December 1979, Figueiredo decided to abolish the two-party system with the help of the National Congress. He forced them to reform their structures, thus allowing new parties to emerge. New social groups began to be formed that called for more liberalization and the end of military rule. These were mostly left-wing groups, a broad alliance ranging from moderate social democrats to more radical socialists who advocated for the proletariat's rise to power.

Forty-eight million Brazilians took to the polls for the 1982 midterm elections. For the first time since the 1960s, state governors and local legislature were elected by direct ballot. The opposition thus emerged victorious in the crucial southern states of Minas Gerais, Rio de Janeiro, and São Paulo, giving it much-needed motivation even though the Democratic Social Party (PDS), the successor to the regime's old ARENA, won a majority in both chambers of the National Congress.

The Workers' Party, or *Partido dos Trabalhadores* (PT), was among the most active opposition groups, and it began working with other political parties to create a unified front against the regime. It began advocating for direct presidential elections, something that could only be achieved by a two-thirds constitutional majority in the Congress. A respective constitutional amendment was drafted and put to the vote, but the PDS-dominated national legislature rejected it.

The 1985 elections proceeded in a volatile political climate. The existing disputes among the members of the regime resulted in unfavorable pre-election conditions. President Figueiredo had favored Colonel Mário Andreazza as his successor, who ultimately lost the nomination to former São Paulo Governor Paulo Maluf, supported by more conservative members of the PDS. This, ultimately, caused a split inside the party. Many members left the PDS, giving the upper hand to the opposition. This included José Sarney, the former president of ARENA and a long-time member of the ruling regime. Sarney became the new leader of the Liberal National Front, comprised of former PDS dissident members. He became a running mate of the opposition's Tancredo Neves, a veteran of Brazilian politics before the military dictatorship and the acting governor of Minas Gerais, who ran for the Brazilian Democratic Movement (MDB).

Together, the Neves-Sarney ballot emerged victorious in the 1985 presidential elections, accruing over 70 percent of the votes and decisively defeating the government's nominee, Paulo Maluf. It was a decisive defeat for the regime, which lost the presidential elections by 300 votes in the electoral college, only winning in two states. The twenty-one-year military dictatorship in Brazil thus ended, only the second instance in the history of Brazil when the sitting government transferred power peacefully to a new president. Unfortunately, there were additional hurdles for the opposition. Before he could be inaugurated into office in March, president-elect Neves fell ill and underwent an emergency operation in Brasilia. Sarney was inaugurated in his stead on March 15. Though this was supposed to be temporary, Neves' health continued to decline, leading to his death on April 21.

Neves was mourned by the public, who feared what could happen with the death of their new leader at such a critical moment. This sentiment was especially prominent because Vice President Sarney, who acted out Neves' term until 1990, was a former member of the old military dictatorship. However, these fears did not materialize. Sarney honored the promises he had made during their campaign and appointed ministers that Neves had favored.

Sarney's first year as president marked the legalization of all political parties, including the Brazilian Communist Party, which had long been outlawed from Brazilian politics. By then, however, it had lost its prestige and mass support, with most Brazilians happily supporting the moderate center-left PT. He followed it up with the ambitious Cruzado Plan—a set of economic measures to fight soaring inflation in the country, including price regulation. The plan, despite a brief period of initial success, ultimately failed, resulting in an increase in Brazil's trade deficit by 1987 and a shortage of supplies.

The following year, a new constitution finally ended the legitimized authoritarian practices of the military government. The new constitution reaffirmed personal and social liberties but was subject to criticism for its ambiguity in reorganizing the federalist system, which had been a staple of Brazilian democracy for a long time. Nevertheless, Sarney's accession as president marked the end of the more than a decade-long struggle to democratize in Brazil. In an international context, it was part of a large wave of democratization throughout the world. In Latin America, Brazil provided an example for the end of authoritarian regimes in Chile and Argentina, while the global democratization process culminated with the fall of the Soviet Union.

In 1989, Brazil had its first direct presidential elections since 1960. Fernando Collor de Mello from the National Reconstruction Party emerged victorious over PT's candidate, Luiz Inacio da Silva (Lula). He became the next president of the country with about thirty-six million votes from the public, while Lula amassed about thirty-one million. Collor won with a neoliberal platform that called for the reduction of government spending and continued to battle the country's severe economic difficulties throughout his term. Although he had been a vocal critic of the existing corruption in Brazilian politics, he was accused of partaking in corruption schemes during his presidency, leading to his impeachment by the Chamber of Deputies in 1992. When his case went up for discussion in the Senate, it became clear he would be convicted, impeached, and disqualified from running again for public office for a time. This prompted Collor to resign from his position, and Vice President Itamar Franco to become acting president for the next two years.

Since the reestablishment of democracy, Brazil has struggled to keep up with the rapidly modernizing world and a globalized society. To this day, the country is plagued with one of the most unequal wealth and income distributions in the world. This resulted in Lula becoming the first ever left-wing president of Brazil in 2002 and his subsequent reelection in 2006, as Brazil experimented with social democracy.

The PT emerged victorious in the 2010 elections as well, leading to the election of the nation's first female president—Dilma Rousseff. She was also reelected in 2014 but was impeached following her involvement in corruption scandals and the increased spending that characterized her tenure as president. "Operation Car Wash"—the investigation that ultimately uncovered the widespread corruption in which many of Brazil's former top politicians were actively involved—was a hit to the prestige of the PT.

The impeachment of Rousseff led to the election of Jair Bolsonaro in 2018, a far-right populist leader from the Social Liberal Party. Bolsonaro's accession as president marked the return of populism to Brazil, part of a wider tendency for world democracies to turn to right-wing populist leaders. Despite his victory, Bolsonaro's policies were widely unpopular both domestically and internationally, especially as his term coincided with the COVID pandemic. He did not effectively deal with the problems caused by the pandemic, including a severe economic crisis, and was also accused of anti-vaccine propaganda campaigns that worsened public health during the most pressing time for the country. Ultimately, his presidency was also marked with several major scandals.

In the 2022 presidential elections, the two-time former president Lula managed to clinch elections with just 50.90 percent of the total votes, making it the closest in the country's history.

Conclusion

Once an unknown promised land on the edge of the known world, Brazil now stands as the fifth largest country in the world by area and the seventh largest in population. It is also the eleventh largest economy with a total national GDP of nearly two trillion USD. Since its discovery and colonization, Brazil has certainly come a long way to its current position. Its journey from pre-colonial times to the present is like that of many other Latin American nations. Still, there is an aura of uniqueness when it comes to Brazil, especially compared to other post-colonial countries on the continent.

The history of Brazil is a history of the strong personalities who dominated the political landscape of the country since the colonial era. Their interests and conflicts shaped the social structures that are still prevalent today and influence not only how the world perceives Brazil, but also how Brazilians perceive themselves. And yet, one thing that perhaps best characterizes Brazilian history is the struggle of the people. Often neglected for the interests of their leaders, they nevertheless continued to fight for their rights, fundamental freedoms, and prosperity— which they deserved, above all.

It is fascinating to see that Brazil has become one of the most diverse countries in the world, with a unique culture that combines the best of the many different peoples that inhabit it. Brazil is known for its hospitality and exciting way of life, which captivates visitors to this day.

The dark memory of oppression, including the practice of slavery, which lasted until the late nineteenth century and cost the lives of millions of innocent people, lives on today. Inequality between the different parts of society can clearly be observed by those who witness the favelas in Rio, and it is only after closely examining the history of the country that the structural reasons behind these inequalities can be identified.

It is Brazilian history that can provide explanations and even solutions to many of the deeply rooted systemic problems that plague Brazil to this day. The aim of this book was to highlight the key developments where these answers can be found and provide insight to readers of all ages and tastes into the captivating history of such a remarkable country as Brazil.

Part 2: Brazilian Mythology

Enthralling Folktales, Vibrant Folklore, Mythical Legends, and Deities of Brazil

Introduction

Most of northern Brazil, approximately 40 percent of the country, is veined by the Amazon Basin. The Amazon River, which flows from west to east from the Andes, runs through eight countries but mostly through Brazil and Peru. The river ends in the Atlantic Ocean at Marajó Bay, Brazil. The Amazon River has the largest volume of water of any river in the world and the biggest drainage system. This vast, extensive region is roughly 2.72 million square miles (6.9 million square kilometers) in size, and the climate is tropical and hot (around 70 to 90°F or 21 to 32°C) with a high volume of rainfall (60 to 200 inches or 150 to 500 centimeters) year-round.

Two-thirds of the Amazon Basin is covered with vast forests of lush, hardwood trees. In the Amazon rainforest, more than forty thousand plant species grow. There are 2.5 million different insect species, 3,000 fish species, some 1,300 bird species, and 427 types of mammals. It is the most biologically diverse place on Earth.

The Amazon rainforest is sometimes referred to as the "lungs of the earth," and for good reason. The lush and diverse flora takes in carbon dioxide and emits at least 6 percent of the world's oxygen. (Historically, the figure was much greater—20 percent—but recent studies suggest photosynthetic organisms that live in the ocean provide a larger proportion of oxygen in the earth's atmosphere than had been originally understood.)

The heavy, wide crowns of the immensely tall trees (many of them measuring 150 to 200 feet or 45 to 60 meters) form the closed canopy that shields the forest from most of the sunlight. Their branches provide habitats for tree frogs, snakes, monkeys (including the buffy-headed marmoset and the crested capuchin, which are indigenous only to Brazil), an incredible range of birds, and invertebrates, including spiders and insects (beetles, moths, bees, wasps, ants, termites, and butterflies). Although the rainforest soil is relatively poor, it provides perfect conditions for alligators, larger snakes like anacondas and boa constrictors, and animals like capybaras, jaguars, and sloths.

In the slow-flowing river channels and lakes, there are manatees, freshwater dolphins, and turtles, although their numbers have been seriously depleted due to being hunted for their meat. There are also several species of piranhas and electric eels. This rich and diverse flora and fauna, so much of it unique to the region, has given rise to many stories and myths throughout the ages.

The very discovery of the Amazon by Europeans was the result of chasing an elusive myth. Francisco de Orellana, a Spanish conquistador and explorer who had assisted his cousin, Francisco Pizarro, in taking possession of Peru, set out on an expedition led by Pizarro's half-brother to explore the regions to the east of Quito. In April 1542, he took a two-masted sailing ship ahead of the main party for provisions and reached the junction of the Napo and Marañón Rivers. Realizing it would be foolhardy to attempt to return due to the current, he drifted with the tide until he reached the mouth of the Amazon in August. When he finally returned to Spain (after a brief sojourn in Trinidad), he had remarkable stories to tell.

He spoke of El Dorado, which is thought to be a reference to the ancient culture of the Muisca people, who offered copious quantities of gold to a lagoon near Bogotá, Colombia, during inauguration ceremonies for new chiefs. The newly appointed chief sailed across the blue waters on a golden raft covered in honey and gold dust, which must have been quite a spectacle if Orellana really witnessed it.

Orellana also told of an attack by a tribe of warrior women that resembled the fabled Amazons of classical Greek literature. They might have been a beardless tribe firing at the ship from the banks of the river at a distance; he and his men just mistook them for women.

Orellana was keen to return to make another exploration of this huge river that had become known as the Amazon after the mythical Greek tribe, but Spain and Portugal were in a bitter dispute over ownership of the lands. The king refused to fund such a voyage but offered some unofficial assistance. Orellana's return to South America was a disaster from the start. He lost ships and men crossing the Atlantic from Spain, and when he finally returned to the Amazon, his ship capsized, and he drowned.

Rumors of a wonderful city of gold captured the interest of European explorers, who were already enamored with the new and exotic South American lands. They scrambled to make expeditions in Colombia, Venezuela, Guyana, and northern Brazil, promising the possibility of immense wealth to their patrons. Sir Walter Raleigh made two such voyages for Queen Elizabeth I of England, and Iberian conquistadors continued their searches, but no such city was ever found. It wasn't until the beginning of the 19th century that the rumor was finally dismissed as a myth.

Even the name Brazil may stem from a myth. Pedro Álvares Cabral, the first European to lead an expedition to Brazil, named the region Ilha de Vera Cruz ("Island of the True Cross") in 1500. It was later discovered that the region was not an island, and it began to be known as Terra de Santa Cruz ("Land of the Holy Cross"). It began to be called Brazil sometime in the 16th century. This name was derived from the redwood tree *paubrasilia*. Its crimson timber was said to be the color of *brasa* (Latin for "embers") and proved a strong wood able to bear heavy loads. It was also known for being particularly attractive. It quickly became an extremely valuable resource, and the wood was shipped back to Portugal for building and for the red dye that could be extracted from its bark.

However, there has been some suggestion (namely in an essay by the author J. R. R. Tolkien) that the country of Brazil might have been named after the mythical and elusive island of Hy-Brasil. It is supposedly only visible through the mists every seven years and is said to be somewhere west of Ireland in the Atlantic Ocean, but this has been dismissed as a fanciful thought by etymologists.

The modern country of Brazil is the fifth largest in the world after Russia, China, Canada, and the United States. It covers a massive area, so it should come as no surprise that it was home to many different tribal groups. It is estimated that when Cabral and his fleet chanced upon Brazil, some two thousand tribes, between two and five million people, lived there. Most of them were semi-nomadic, and they lived in coastal areas or by rivers where fish were plentiful, and they could cultivate plants for food.

It is believed their ancestors originally migrated fifteen thousand years earlier from Asia over the Bering Strait. From there, they gradually moved south through North America. Over the years, the indigenous people began to form myths about the land around them. As the centuries passed, these myths transformed due to colonization, conversion to Christianity, and slavery. European ideas, particularly religion, impacted the characters found in ancient tales. Different messages would be told, and the newer generations passed on the altered version, with the original often being lost to time.

Today, Brazil is seen as a creative, vibrant country with a strong identity despite its population being of such diverse heritage. It is a country associated with sports, particularly football or soccer, samba, carnivals, cuisine, and literature.

Brazil's outstanding literary tradition carries on what was done by the ancient settlers. In recent times, it tends to deal with themes of social and racial injustice. Elements from the country's rich mythology are referenced and echoed in poetry and novels crafted by writers who are familiar with these traditions.

Chapter One – The Creation Myths

Brazilian stories of how the world and humanity came to be are as varied and diverse as its people and landscapes. Some of these myths are lost, incomplete, or have been changed through the ages, but those that remain give a fascinating insight into Brazilian cultures and communities.

The Tupi people inhabited some three-quarters of the coastal regions of Brazil when the Portuguese arrived at the beginning of the 16th century. They were accomplished farmers and grew a variety of vegetables and legumes. Although they were divided into numerous individual tribes, ranging from three hundred to two thousand people, they shared a common language. The Portuguese settlers found the Tupi to have no discernible religion, but there were myths and legends that the colonizers perhaps overlooked in their enthusiasm to bring these people under the wing of Christianity.

The Tupi told stories of a god named Nhanderuvuçu. He was the principal god and the creator. He destroyed everything that had come before and then produced two souls from which he created everything: the world, the air, and the water. He unraveled chaos to bring order, which brought the other Tupi deities into being.

One of these was Tupã, the god of thunder and the skies. One day, he released two birds into the sky. One was Guaraci, the sun god. He was responsible for all living things during daylight. The other bird, Jaci, became the moon and oversaw all living things at night.

In another version, Tupã only created Guaraci. He was exhausted from endlessly overseeing the world. So, Tupã made him a sister whose lunar gleam would prevent the world from descending into complete darkness while the sun god slept. When Guaraci saw her, he was dazzled by her beauty and welcomed the opportunity to sleep so he could wake up and be captivated by her all over again.

Guaraci asked Tupã to convey his deep admiration for Jaci. Tupã formed Rudá, the god of love and affection, to take these messages to Jaci while the lovelorn sun god slept.

Jaci was in the rainforest when she finally met her brother Guaraci. She was just as mesmerized by his golden, glittering magnificence as he was with her, and as the two gazed upon each other, Guaraci's fiery passion threatened to set the earth ablaze. Jaci's tears of love and happiness almost caused the earth to flood. They realized they could never be together, so they reluctantly parted.

Feckless Guaraci soon forgot all about his lunar love since she took great care never to appear until he was asleep. However, Jaci remained heartbroken. Her tears fell to the earth and down the mountains, eventually forming the mighty Amazon River.

Jaci was the most beautiful and benevolent of all the divine beings. She was responsible for plants and reproduction. Despite her loveliness, she found herself isolated and lonely, pining for her beloved in the cool night sky. So, from time to time, she would choose a pure young woman to join her in the heavens as a star.

One girl, called Naiá, longed to join Jaci and become one of her celestial maidens. She wandered in the forest clearings and the mountains, searching for the moon in the hopes of persuading her, but she could never find her. As time passed, Naiá refused to eat. Preoccupied with her search, she began to waste away.

One evening, she awoke to see the moon reflected in a lake. As if in a dream, she threw herself into the water with her arms outstretched as if to embrace the moon and drowned.

Jaci saw what happened and was moved by the girl's sacrifice. She decided to grant her a unique honor, allowing her to live forever between the water and the skies. Naiá was made into the "water star," the Amazonian water lily (*Victoria amazonica* or *Vitória-Régia*), a giant white flower that lasts just forty-eight hours. It opens its milky white petals on the first night and then changes color to a purplish red when it opens again on the second night. This is Naiá opening her arms to bathe in the moon's light.

In the period when day turns into night, women traditionally ask Jaci to protect their men who leave on nocturnal hunting trips. She encourages these hunters to hurry home to their wives by reawakening their love for them while they are away. In some versions of this story, the god of love, Rudá, was accompanied by Cairé, the full moon, and Caitití, the new moon. These were the times when lovers should unite.

The Tupi god of the underworld was Anhangá, who was also the protector of animals. Ceuci was the goddess of the fields and dwellings, and Sumé was the god of agriculture and discipline.

The Guaraní people are another indigenous group in South America. They are distinguished from the Tupi people by their use of the Guaraní language and were more prominent in the southern regions of Brazil, Paraguay, Argentina, and Bolivia. Their creation myth begins with Tupã being married to the moon goddess Arasy. With her help, he came down to Earth to create everything: the seas, the rivers, the forests, and the mountains. Next came all living things and, finally, Tau, the spirit of evil, and Angatupyry, the spirit of goodness.

The first humans created by Tupã were Rupave and Sypave. Tupã was good to them and helped them learn essential life skills, such as hunting, building shelters, and how certain plants could be used to eat or heal. He encouraged them to have many children together. Their second son, Marangatú, became a great leader of humankind. He had a beautiful daughter named Kerana. When the evil spirit Tau saw the lovely Kerana, he was determined to have her. So, he transformed himself into a handsome stranger in order to seduce her. However, when he arrived at her home, Angatupyry was waiting for him, having realized his ill intent.

For seven days, the good and evil spirits battled until Tau was defeated, and good prevailed. Pytajovái, the god of valor and warriors, exiled him. All seemed well until evil Tau returned in the dead of night and abducted Kerana.

Together, Tau and Kerana had seven sons, but Arasy was appalled at Kerana's abduction and cursed all of them. They became hideous beings. The oldest was Teju Jagua, a giant lizard with seven dog heads whose eyes burned with fire. Tupã managed to tame him and made him the spirit of caves. He only ate fruit and honey and lived a quiet life, guarding treasure found in caverns. Teju Jagua was almost immobile because of the weight of his many dog heads. He rolled around in his dark subterranean dwellings so that fragments of gold, silver, and colored gems stuck to his scaly skin.

The second son, Mbói Tu'ĩ ("snake parrot"), became a huge serpent with a parrot's head and a blood-red forked tongue. His head was covered with feathers, and his violent squawk could be heard from miles away. Anyone who came across him was destined for bad luck. He became the protector of all aquatic creatures and swamplands.

Moñái, the third son of Tau and Kerana, became the god of the air and open fields. He had the writhing body of a snake and two antennae-like horns on his head. His gaze was mesmerizing and hypnotic, and he coiled around trees to capture birds, which he ate.

Jasy Jateré, the fourth son, is often described as a sort of goblin or gnome. His name means "small piece of moon," and this was manifested in his lustrous pale hair. He had startling blue eyes and often carried a magical staff. He wore a hat, but he was naked otherwise. His hat enhanced his powers, which were unpleasant and disturbing. He whistled like a bird to attract children, and then he kidnapped them. He would take them to a remote mountain area where he played with them and fed them honey or sweet fruits. Then, as he prepared to leave them, he licked or kissed them, leaving them deaf, suffering seizures, or giving them some other long-term debilitating condition. In some versions, he preferred to drown the unfortunate child. The Guaraní people said he could be rendered helpless if he was plied with drink and if his staff was taken from him. If this happened, he would sob pitifully, just like one of the children he had lured away.

In other versions of Jasy Jateré's story, he searches for children who will not take a nap. As such, he was made the spirit of the siesta and guardian of the yerba mate, a plant native to South America that can be steeped in water to make a drink comparable to tea. This drink was extremely popular with the Guaraní and some Tupi communities before the colonization of the region. In these tales, Jasy Jateré was a useful cautionary villain for warning children who refused to take their afternoon nap.

Kurupi, the fifth son, was the spirit of fertility, sexuality, and lust. Another short being with a human-like appearance, he was hairy and ugly and had an extremely long penis. His penis was so long that he had to wind it around his waist several times like a belt. He was often found lurking in the forest, his movements clumsy and ungainly, perhaps due to the discomfort of his bizarre deformity. He would assault any woman who dared to walk there alone. She would be left dead or pregnant after his attentions. At nighttime, he dared to steal into villages. His penis was able to negotiate its way through doors, windows, and other openings, allowing him to find a way to sleeping women whom he impregnated.

Many unexplained pregnancies (unmarried women and some who had not had relations with their husbands) were blamed on Kurupi. Children he was supposed to have fathered were expected to resemble him. They would be short, dark, ugly, and hairy. Sometimes, children who fit that description were teased, with others saying they were Kurupi's sons or daughters.

The most violent and savage son, Ao Ao, was a sheeplike creature with huge claws and enormous fangs, which he used to tear into human flesh. He has also been compared to a peccary, the porcine South American mammal that can be more aggressive than a sheep, especially when protecting its territory or young. Ao Ao was named after the dreadful howl he made, which alerted people to his presence. Once he had honed in on a victim, the only way to escape was to climb one of the palm trees sacred to the Guaraní.

Ao Ao was fed children abducted by his brother Jasy Jateré from time to time, and he is also associated with reproduction, as he fathered several children.

The seventh and youngest son, Luison (or sometimes Lobizón), was a kind of wolf man. In his earliest incarnation, he represented death since he feasted on rotting meat and skulked around burial grounds and cemeteries. If one felt the cold touch of his paw, they would die soon after.

Fortunately for the Guaraní people, they did not need to fear this foul family forever. These seven brothers had a story about their demise. The third of the brothers, the serpent Moñái, was a very crafty thief. He robbed villages and hid his spoils in a cave. The communities he stole from blamed one another for his raids and bitterly fought against each other until they realized who the real thief was. A beautiful young woman, Porâsí, offered to help put an end to his misdemeanors and his vile brothers at the same time. She flirted with Moñái and managed to persuade him that she had fallen in love with him. Before they could marry, she asked to meet his brothers.

She stayed with Teju Jagua as Moñái went to gather his brothers for the ceremony. When they all reunited in the oldest brother's cave, Porâsí ensured each of them had plenty to drink. Soon, they were completely inebriated. She tried to sneak away with the intention of sealing the cave shut with a large stone, leaving the horrible brothers inside, but Moñái grabbed her. She screamed to alert the people waiting outside with the great stone and told them to close the cave with her inside, sacrificing herself.

The monstrous sons of Tau and Kerana were no more. Angatupyry raised the soul of the courageous Porâsí from the dark cave where she had died and made her into the morning star to remind the people of her sacrifice.

The Xingu people, who today inhabit part of Mato Grosso, a state in central Brazil to the south of the Amazon rainforest, tell a sad story about the creation of the first man, Mavutsinim, who lived all alone. He was desperately lonely until he transformed a shell (or a clam) into a woman and married her. In time, they had a son. Mavutsinim took him away to travel and hunt with him. The boy's mother was devastated. She wept inconsolably and returned to her lagoon to become a shell again. This story is often viewed as an allegory for the circle of life, particularly for women. She is born, leaves the family home for marriage and motherhood, feels a great loss when her children grow and leave the home, and then eventually dies. Mavutsinim's thoughtlessness or cruelty toward his shell-wife is a portent of the misogyny women faced in less enlightened ages.

In the state of Pará, located in northern Brazil, the indigenous Arará people speak of Akuanduba, their creator. He existed at a time when the sky and water were separated only by a small shell. At that time, humans were the stars in the sky and led a simple existence eating, drinking, and sleeping. Whenever these star people began to eat, drink, or sleep to excess, they would upset the natural balance, and Akuanduba would play his magical flute so order could be restored.

Because humans lack self-discipline and common sense and cannot see what is best for them, this peaceful existence came to an end when the star people selfishly started stealing from one another. This escalated into so much rage and resentment they could not, or rather would not, hear the conciliatory notes from Akuanduba's flute. The sky broke, and the moon and all of the star people fell into the water.

The elderly star folk and the young children drowned or died from the impact of the fall. The birds were alarmed to see this disaster unfold, and a curica (a parrot) managed to get hold of the moon and dragged it back into the heavens. A small indentation said to be left by its beak can still be seen on the moon's surface at times. Parrots swooped over the water, picked up some of the surviving people, and returned them to the skies, where they continued to exist as stars.

However, the water was full of evil spirits, and the surviving people began to experience misery that they had never experienced as stars under Akuanduba's guardianship. He had lost interest in helping them and had transformed himself into a terrible black jaguar that stalked the people.

Eventually, the people managed to form a community with help from the creatures of the land. The sloths taught them to feast, and the macaws stole fire for them. They discovered the edible animals and plants in the forest and learned how to build and weave. They even made flutes so they could make music and sing like they had when they were stars in the sky.

The Arará developed into great warriors and hunters, and they always remained grateful and respectful toward the birds that saved them. The name Arará means "people of the red macaws" (the Tupi word for macaw is *ará*).

The Yanomami indigenous ethnic group from the northern region of the state of Amazonas speak of a birdlike god named Omam (or Omai) who created the world. He maintained and repaired it by adding layers of nature, such as the clouds, the sky, and the seas. When he was satisfied, he went fishing in the ocean to appreciate what he had made. There, he found a woman. When he had "freed" her sexual organs using piranha teeth, he made her the mother of all the people.

The Baniwa people, who live by the Içana River on the borders of Brazil, Colombia, and Venezuela, have an extremely complex myth about the origin of the world. At the beginning of time, the earth was very small, and all of the animals and people lived in chaos. The animals were wild and savage. One day, the Lord of All the Animals devoured one of the people and then tossed one of its finger bones into the river.

An old woman related to this person wept so bitterly for her loss that the Lord of All the Animals (sometimes called Enumhere) allowed her to go and get this bone. Inside it were three tiny shrimp called the Nhiãperikuli ("He inside the bone"). The old woman took the bone to her home and nurtured it. The shrimp transformed into crickets. As she fed them, they started to sing and grow. Under her care, they grew larger each day and eventually developed into humans.

These Nhiãperikuli began to change the world. They introduced order, and when they were ready, they took vengeance on the wild animals that had devoured the old woman's family.

The Lord of All the Animals was furious with this new world, but he slyly concealed his true feelings and asked the brothers to help him establish a garden. While they were surveying the area, he set fire to the edges of the land. Soon, there was a huge blaze. Each brother bored a hole into one of the embaúba trees and got inside them. When the flames reached these trees, they exploded, and the Nhiãperikuli flew into the air. This made them immortal.

The three brothers had a son together named Kuwai. His body was full of holes and encased all of the natural elements of the world. Amaru, the "first" woman (the old woman who nurtured the Nhiãperikuli apparently didn't count), appeared at around the same time.

Inside Kuwai was everything that makes the world as it is, the sights, sounds, smells, and tastes. As these things were released from him, the world grew into its actual size. As well as populating the earth with every known element—spirits, animals, diseases, songs, and the sounds of the forest—he turned to the people and explained the nature of existence to them.

At this point, this common origin story becomes intertwined with the myth of another major character of Brazilian mythology, Jurupari. However, in the Baniwa people's tradition, Kuwai turned into a monster to devour three disobedient boys who had broken their initiation process by eating roasted nuts. Afterward, the Nhiãperikuli pushed Kuwai into an inferno, which made the earth contract into its smaller size again.

The shamans, or *pajé*, of the region recount that this was by no means the end of Kuwai. He retreated to the center of the world to become the Lord of Sickness. All of the diseases, illnesses, and poor health conditions generated from his earthly remains and poisoned the environment. His spirit body was covered in thick black fur like the sloth. When he encountered the souls of the sick, he encased them in his arms—in the same manner as the sloth—and squeezed the breath from them as the *pajés* frantically negotiated with him in the hope he would allow their unfortunate patient to continue living.

From the ashes of the huge fire that had destroyed the physical presence of Kuwai, the people found sacred pipes and trumpets. The Nhiãperikuli directed the men to play these instruments in sacred ceremonies, but the women grew envious and stole them. As they fled, they played the pipes, and the world opened up again. Nhiãperikuli and the men, in the form of wild animals, hunted them down to take back the instruments.

Afterward, the Nhiãperikuli produced a group of people from the Aiari River. These would be the ancestors of the human race.

The universe, in this Baniwa myth system, is divided into multiple layers, from four (Wapinakwa, "The Place of Bones," Hekwapi, "This World," Apakwa Hekwapi, "The Other World," and Apakwa Eenu, "The Sky of the Other World") to twenty-five: twelve above the human plain and twelve below. Kuwai is placed (by the *pajé*) with the other spirits they share contact with, such as the bird spirits that help them to find lost souls somewhere in Apakwa Eenu.

The Nhiãperkuli remained the supreme being. They were responsible for the heart of the world and existed in Dio, a heavenly plain where there is no suffering or sickness. With them lives Kamathawa, the harpy eagle, a symbol that has come to represent shamans and *pajé* throughout South America.

Kamathawa is regarded as a sentinel tasked with guarding Nhiãperkuli's wisdom and sacred medicine knowledge held in crystals. In traditional ceremonies, *pajé* use harpy eagle feathers to sweep and clear the skies in order to see into these crystals and influence the weather when the rainy season becomes excessive.

Some people believe Kamathawa is the younger brother of the Nhiãperkuli and that he was killed by some malevolent beings. As they prepared to eat his body (having turned it into a large catfish), the Nhiãperkuli turned into a wasp and managed to retrieve Kamathawa's heart, which it cooked. As the boiling water bubbled and foamed, hawks began to fly out of it, each larger than the one before. Finally, the great harpy eagle emerged and flew in circles overhead.

The Nhiãperkuli gave this eagle Kamathawa great logs to carry. After regaining his strength, he avenged himself by killing and eating the enemies who had killed him in his previous form.

The Desana (or Dessana) people from the Rio Negro Basin believed all humans were descended from one being, Yebá Bëló, the "grandmother of the universe." She appeared from nowhere and lived in a marvelous glowing structure made from quartz. Other tribal myths describe her creating the sun and people from her chewed ipadu leaves (the leaves of the coca, a herbal plant used as a stimulant and in medicine). In another version, she took a tobacco seed from her left breast and fertilized it with milk from her right breast to form the earth.

She created five thunder men who were supposed to make the first human beings, but when they failed, Yebá Bëló made Yebá Gõãmu, the "Great Grandson of the World" and then his brother, Umukomahsu Boreka.

The two set off with the third thunder man to create humankind. The thunder man transformed himself into a serpent and slipped into the Lake of Milk until he reached the bottom. Then, as a canoe, he took the brothers to this enchanted place, and they took all the precious things they could find in the world. They built dwellings, and their precious things transformed into people. Yebá Gõãmu breathed life into them. The thunder man directed these first men to go and take a leaf from the ipadu tree and eat it. When they felt pain in their bellies, they were told to light a fire stick and dip it in a gourd of water before drinking it. Then, they should vomit in a very specific place. Once this had been completed, the first men saw they had produced two beautiful women. These people would be the common ancestors of all humanity.

The thunder man's canoe carried all of the people who had been created to the surface of the lake. They stepped onto land near a waterfall. Yebá Gõãmu remained on the canoe to create the chiefs of the first six tribes, including Boreka, the chief of the Desana. He gave each of them certain powers and enchanted treasures so that their people would live harmoniously as neighbors.

Tellingly, the seventh being he created was the white man, born with a rifle in his hand. Yebá Gõãmu did not give him any other gifts—he said he had no need of them. Yebá Gõãmu knew he was fearless and ruthless and that he would start wars in order to steal what he wanted from others. As this white man left the lake, he fired his gun and, without looking back, set off toward the sun, ready to take whatever he wanted by force.

The Kamayurá, from the northeast of Brazil near the mouth of the Amazon, relate how there was no light at the beginning, as the sun's rays were limited to the kingdom of birds in the sky. The people who existed on the earth lived in eternal darkness until the sun god, Kuat, wondered why his glorious light didn't benefit everyone.

The moon god, Iae, told him it was because Urubutsin, the two-headed king of the vultures, had taken possession of it and knitted the tree canopies together so tightly that he could keep it exclusively for the birds.

Kuat and Iae resolved to trick Urubutsin, and they persuaded the king of the flies to take the effigy of a body to the banks of the Amazon and fill it with maggots. The buzzing of the flies gained the notice of Urubutsin. Looking down from his lofty perch, he could see the effigy had bright, gleaming eyes. He and his subjects flew down to investigate, and upon finding the juicy maggots, they gorged on them with relish.

Kuat and Iae had hidden themselves in the effigy of another body. When Urubutsin approached it, they grabbed hold of his foot and refused to let go. All of Urubutsin's cowardly subjects quickly flew away, leaving him with little option but to negotiate for his freedom. After some discussion, a deal was agreed. The light would be shared, but each evening, darkness would prevail, and the moon would watch over the world.

A creation myth that came from the African Candomblé religion, which was brought to Brazil by West African enslaved people and intermingled with Christianity, is the story of Iemanjá.

This tale begins in a world of perpetual light. There was no sunrise or sunset, no nocturnal creatures, or no cool nighttime. There was only hot, bright sunlight.

The goddess Iemanjá lived deep in the sea. One of her daughters fell in love with one of the men who lived on the land and left her mother to marry him. At first, she was very happy and loved her husband and her glittering new surroundings. But after some time, the endless glare of the sun became too much for her and made her eyes hurt and her head ache. She longed to go back to her mother, where the dark, cool waters would soothe her.

Her husband was very concerned to see his wife so unhappy and sick. So, when she told him of Iemanjá's kingdom, he sent three of his men to beg the goddess for some of the cool darkness for his wife.

The men traveled the perilous journey under the water and finally reached Iemanjá's realm. They prostrated themselves before her, begging for some of the darkness their master's wife craved. As soon as the goddess realized her daughter was suffering, she gave them a large bag of her underwater darkness and told them to take it to her quickly but warned them not to open it because she had filled it with night spirits. Only her daughter would be able to control them.

The three men dragged the bag through the water and onto the land. Once there, the bag began to make strange sounds. As they carried it on their heads, they began to grow frightened. The night spirits' screeches and howls were like nothing they had heard before.

The first man was so terrified he could not stop shaking. The second suggested they should just dump the bag somewhere and run away. The third man suggested if they had a quick peek inside the bag, they would see what was making the dreadful noises and wouldn't be afraid anymore. He carefully unsealed the bag, but before he could take a look, all of the night insects, birds, and creatures swarmed out of it, and the stars sprang into the sky.

The men fled in panic, but fortunately, Iemanjá's daughter was waiting on the shore. She greeted the night spirits. Darkness descended everywhere, and the creatures calmed their noises until there was just a gentle hum. The world felt cool and soft and gleamed in the moonlight.

Iemanjá's daughter fell asleep and awoke feeling soothed and well again. Her husband was delighted to see his wife happy. As nighttime had been established in her new home, Iemanjá's daughter bestowed three gifts to the people of the land. The first was the morning star, so they might see when the night was ending. She then gave the rooster the task of calling each dawn to greet daylight. Finally, the birds agreed they would sing their most beautiful songs each morning to celebrate each new day. This period of the early morning when the sun rises became known as *madrugada*, a special time of renewal and refreshment.

Chapter Two – High Spirits

Many of the indigenous people of Brazil share stories of spirits, apparitions of people who have passed into another world after death or are the essence that makes up the very soul of humans or animals. It is, in some ways, a catch-all term that can include gods, ghosts, and entities with powers beyond the wit and understanding of men and women. Spirits are good, bad, or both at the same time. Sometimes, they are even beyond such arbitrary concepts. A good example of this is the Jurupari cult, which is found among nearly all the indigenous people of northwestern Amazonia and is known by several names, including Yurupary and Kowai. It is particularly prevalent in the Arawakan communities of the Rio Negro and the Uaupés River.

The Tupi Guaraní goddess of crops and dwellings, Ceuci, was originally a lovely young woman who lived in a village where a special tree grew. Tupã had given strict instructions that the women who lived there were forbidden from eating its fruit during their fertile periods.

Ceuci was resting in the shade of the tree one hot day and could not resist trying one of its succulent mapati, a sweet, juicy fruit rather like a grape (or a caimito or cucura, depending on the location of the story). As she bit into it, the juice ran from the flesh down her body and between her thighs.

Soon afterward, she realized she was pregnant. The elders of her community were appalled since she had no husband or partner, and they struggled to understand how she could have conceived a child. They decided to banish her from the village, so Ceuci left to have her baby on her own.

Some versions of this story are more earthy, strange, and graphic. There is the suggestion that Ceuci had been made pregnant through an incestuous relationship with an element, possibly the sun, the moon, or thunder. Since she had no vagina, the birth was only completed when she had been pierced by a particular fish.

She named her son Jurupari, and he was a remarkable, precocious boy. By the age of ten, the elders of the village who had exiled his mother listened to his ideas and recognized the wisdom of his teachings. But young Jurupari, according to different origin stories, had no mouth and existed on tobacco smoke. He was able to communicate by gestures or by making dreadful, frightening noises from holes in his body. He was not always (at least entirely) human; sometimes, he was a monkey with the head of a man or a manifestation of some kind of plant or tree.

Either way, he quickly asserted his influence and helped the people of the village understand the order of nature. He also introduced a series of rituals and rites for the men. He made it very clear that no woman should witness these sacred ceremonies. Ceuci, his mother, could not resist spying on this ceremony even though she knew it was forbidden and punishable by death.

She stole into the village, but as soon as Jurupari and the men had assembled, Tupã sent a lightning bolt, killing her instantaneously. Jurupari was called to her, but he knew she had died because she had violated the sacred rules. He prayed to Tupã to reward her for her devotion to her son and her exemplary motherhood. Suddenly, her body appeared to be filled with light as it rose from the ground and into the heavens, where it became the brightest star in the Pleiades constellation. It remained there, Jurupari told his people sagely, to remind them to respect the laws he was introducing.

Jurupari is an unusual character in Brazilian mythology. Despite all of his promise in Ceuci's story, he is generally known as the demon of dreams and an omen of bad fortune. In some legends, he is a malevolent and evil presence that sometimes suffocates people as they struggle to awake from nightmares.

The people of the Upper Xingu recount how Jurupari overhauled the male initiation ceremony, introducing fine costumes and new rituals. The boys who were ready to join the cult were sent to collect fruit for the proceedings. Although they were warned not to eat any of them, they disobeyed these instructions and roasted and ate some of them. Jurupari was furious. He called to the heavens and created a terrible thunderstorm, during which the boys ran to find shelter in a cave they had found. Unfortunately for them, it was actually Jurupari's mouth. (In some stories, it was his anus.) Jurupari quickly devoured them all.

One of the younger and smaller boys was too late to enter the "cave." He alone survived to tell the tale. Having heard of the dreadful fate that had befallen their sons, the parents of the disobedient boys vowed to take their revenge and planned to kill Jurupari. Replete from his dinner of the young men, Jurupari had gone to rest in the mountains (or the sky), but when the villagers offered him some of the fine liquor they had distilled, he couldn't resist joining the party.

When he arrived that evening, he vomited the remains of the boys he had eaten into large baskets of fruit that had been prepared for the feast and then joined the villagers, dancing and singing while consuming copious quantities of their exotic and potent drink.

But as the sun came over the horizon, the people threw him onto a fire, knowing it was the only way they could kill him. Although he was no more (other than his nightly activities as a sleep demon), the ashes of his flesh created a whole host of unpleasantness: snakes, stinging ants, and lots of other poisonous creatures. The ashes of his skeleton also brought forth the paxiúba palm, the huge "walking tree" that appears to rise from its exposed, tentacle-like roots.

Pipes were crafted from these roots, and the haunting music they produced was thenceforth Jurupari's voice. The other elements used in the rituals (such as beeswax and tobacco) were said to be his tongue, brain, and other organs.

Sometime later, the sun ordered the men to perform Jurupari's ceremony, but they were too lazy and couldn't be bothered to retrieve the paxiúba palm pipes from the water. They slept instead. The women, however, found the instruments and played the sacred music. The sun did not punish them but reversed the natural order in the village. The men did all of the work and had children, while the women dedicated themselves to Jurupari's sacred rituals.

The men found this situation untenable. They attacked the women with whips and brutalized them until they cried out in frustration. Once the men had regained control, the women were made to menstruate as a sign of their submission. It was then (at least in this version of the myth) that the sacred instrument became taboo to the womenfolk. Any woman who tried to play these instruments or even attempted to make anything similar was sentenced to death by poisoning. Once the verdict was passed, the woman was expected to take a lethal draft voluntarily, but if she refused, she was executed.

The Desana people were one of the ethnic groups that practiced the Jurupari initiation rituals that developed from this myth. In the daytime, the women and children were forbidden from entering the village longhouse while the men brought in fruits from the rainforest and played their pipes to express appreciation for nature's bountiful gifts, in particular, plentiful fish. In the evening, the music stopped, and the women were invited in to drink *yagé* (ayahuasca), a traditional hallucinogenic preparation, and dance. Sometimes, the men whipped the women and children to help them grow strong and resilient.

The initiation ceremony for the young men approaching adulthood involved them being given coca leaves (the plant from which cocaine is produced), snuff, and *yagé*. Then, they were whipped. When they were deemed ready, elements said to have been formed from Jurupari's ashes were gathered together to form an approximation of his body. Two men dressed in full ceremonial costume (representing Jurupari) showed them the sacred pipes. After suffering another whipping, they were taken to the river, where water was poured over their heads in a ceremony reminiscent of a baptism.

The young men must then spend several weeks completely independent from the women, learning traditional tasks exclusive to the male community, such as basket weaving and only consuming cold food and drink. This formative period ended with the young men presenting their female relatives with the baskets they had made. A festival would take place, during which these young men drank piping hot drinks and consumed hot chili peppers.

Anhangá, which means "ancient soul," is another god or spirit that is a part of several different people groups' mythologies but is inconsistent in terms of his role and purpose.

In the Tupinambá culture, Anhangá is a shapeshifter who prevents the dead from progressing to the next world. He torments and tortures the living on occasion. His presence was of the greatest concern when a recently deceased body was being prepared with the sacred rites for its journey to Guajupiá, the "Land Without Evils." Offerings were left for

Anhangá beside a fire that had been lit to warm the body of the dead, as well as the food necessary for its sustenance. These fires would continue to be lit for many years by the dead's descendants to help keep those souls safe from the attention of Anhangá.

The Mawé (or Sateré) people native to the Amazon regard Anhangá as a demon with evil intent. They believe he is capable of cursing, abducting, and killing at will. Since Anhangá can take different forms, they rely on his dread of water. They think the spirits that protect the rivers help repel him.

However, in Tupi mythology, Anhangá is a genie of the forest and often appears as a mighty white stag with red eyes that burn and sharpened horns. However, he can also be an armadillo, an ox, an arapaima fish, or even a man. He vigilantly protects his habitat and punishes those who cause harm to it, especially if they harm female creatures and their young. Sometimes, he is invisible and charges at hunters, attacking them physically. Sometimes, he puts them under a spell that makes them crazy. There were rituals to keep him at bay, especially when the Tupi hunters had to go to the forest to feed their people. They left offerings (generally tobacco and liquor) or burned cashew nuts. They also made crosses with wood from the forest trees to deter Anhangá, a practice that was likely heavily influenced by the European colonizers or missionaries.

The most iconic character in Brazilian folklore is the spirit known as Saci or Saci-Pererê. He is not a god or demon; rather, he is a young Black boy with just one leg. He is always seen wearing a red cap and often smokes a pipe. He is a mischievous and cheeky entity who loves to play jokes and tricks for his own amusement.

Saci is quick despite his impairment. He juggles with burning embers, and he can ride a horse or, more often, the tropical whirlwinds known as dust devils. When he appears, cooks find their sugar has been exchanged for salt, there are flies in the soup, and milk has turned sour. Others find their most useful or treasured possessions missing and that needles have lost their sharpness. Strange, alarming animal noises can be heard in the dead of night; it is as if some horrible beast is prowling through the village.

Other people say that his whirling dancing causes the dust devils. If a rosary with each bead individually blessed is thrown into a dust devil, it might be possible to capture Saci. He will then bestow all kinds of favors and luck on his captor on the condition that he is treated well. If Saci is treated cruelly, he will become a vindictive enemy.

If throwing a rosary into a spinning tumult of dirt should prove too difficult, Saci can also be caught in a large sieve. To delay his progress, one can leave a rope full of tight and complicated knots, as this will distract him for several hours. He cannot resist unfastening them, and he will not rest until he has unpicked each and every knot.

Those wanting to endear themselves to Saci leave him gifts, usually tobacco or *cachaça*, a strong liquor made from fermented sugar cane, to avoid his attention. Anyone brave enough to steal Saci's red cap will be granted a wish, but there is a price to pay. The hat has a dreadful, pungent smell that will never leave those who have touched it.

This spirit is most likely to originate from the Ŷaci-Ŷaterê, a Tupi-Guaraní spirit, a one-legged child with eye-catching bright red hair. Just as rascally as Saci, he tricks people with animal calls and shrill whistling, but his activities are restricted to nighttime.

The enslaved African people who were brought to Brazil by the early European settlers readily took to the stories of Ŷaci-Ŷaterê. They enjoyed telling their children about this wicked little sprite who was just naughty enough to enthrall youngsters without terrifying them; life was hard enough already.

Because of this, over time, Saci developed into a Black boy. The red hair became a red cap. Since the elders of the African communities tended to be the storytellers and frequently enjoyed a reed pipe of tobacco as they held court, Saci developed his own smoking habit.

The Portuguese in Brazil compared Saci with the trasgu, a little forest goblin creature dressed in leaves and moss. He has a black face and is also a trickster. Some of Saci's antics might have been heavily influenced by him. There are also similarities to the mythological monopods, dwarf-like creatures with one oversized foot in the center of their bodies. These creatures were described in ancient Greek and Roman literature and were still thought to exist in some medieval etymologies.

As well as being vulnerable to rosary beads, Saci will stop his misbehaving and flee if he sees a crucifix, leaving behind just the faintest whiff of sulfur (an element long associated with the devil in Christian folklore).

In some stories, Saci has the power to control the weather and can appear and disappear at will; his glowing pipe can only be seen by the most observant. He cannot cross water unless he transforms himself into a *matitaperê* (or *matita pereira*), the striped cuckoo.

The classic children's book *O Saci*, written by Montero Lobato in 1921, is an enduring favorite among Brazilian children throughout the country. It tells the story of a young boy, Pedrinho, who lives on a farm in São Paulo. He learns about Saci from his grandfather. He decides to capture him to learn his secrets, and as the two engage in a battle of wits, each trying to outdo the other, they become close friends. They learn important lessons about trust, comradeship, resilience, and respect for the natural world.

A similar impish creature, mostly known in the state of Rio Grande do Sul, is the sanguanel. Although he is said to be harmless, his activities are sinister and worrisome by modern standards.

Thought to have originated from myths shared by Italian immigrants, the sanguanel is a kind of bright red hobgoblin that lives in the forests and mountainous areas. He likes to play pranks and tricks on adults, usually related to his ability to appear and disappear, but he is most interested in very young children and babies. He kidnaps them and hides with them in tall trees or shrubs. While frantic parents search for their missing children, he feeds his little captives on honey and water, which he drips into their mouths from special cups he forms from leaves. When the children are found, they are disoriented and sleepy. They can never quite recall what happened to them while they were in the sanguanel's care.

The sanguanel is supposed to have a twin sister called the sanguanela. She is his opposite in every way. Rather than being red, she has white skin and blonde hair. She prefers vinegar to wine (suggesting, perhaps, that the sanguanel enjoys his liquor) and has some power over water.

Romãozinho is the nasty spirit of a child that was once a human. He was a very bad boy from the start. He relished destroying plants and flowers. As soon as he was old enough, he hunted and killed any living creatures, even the songbirds that make life so pleasant for everyone. He hated everyone and never passed up an opportunity to spread spite, suspicion, and bad feelings. He even loathed his parents and managed to persuade his father that his innocent mother was in love with another man.

One day, his mother asked him to take his father a chicken she had cooked for him while he was working in the fields. Romãozinho ate the whole chicken while he walked. When he eventually reached his father, he handed over the chicken bones and said that was all that was left. His mother and her boyfriend had eaten the rest.

Ramãozinho's father, mad with rage, returned to the family home and struck and killed his poor wife. As she was taking her last breaths, she saw her malevolent son smiling to himself, and she realized that he was behind the terrible fate that had befallen her. Her last act was to place a terrible curse on him: he would never know heaven or hell while a single human remained on Earth.

Her son, though completely remorseless, found himself reduced to wandering the world. He is no longer human, but he plays tricks on people, mainly out of boredom and maliciousness.

It is possible that this myth is a Brazilian interpretation of Ahasvero, a cursed immortal man from 13th-century Europe. He was also left wandering aimlessly for all of time.

In the northeastern states of Brazil, especially in the Sertão area, the spirit of a young woman known as Comadre Fulozinha ("Good Friend Blossom") is said to protect the rainforest. She has long dark hair. It is so thick and lustrous that it can cover her whole body. She is tall and willowy, and she is said to wear a grey diaphanous dress and a red necklace that is so beautiful and intricate that it could not have been made by human hands.

Some communities call her *Mãe da Mata* ("Mother of the Woods") and say flowers grow wherever she has walked. She has a distinctive whistle that becomes quieter as she approaches. Anyone who hears her is advised to leave since she dislikes humans disturbing the forests.

The most common origin story says that Comadre Fulozinha was a caboclo (person of mixed indigenous Brazilian and European descent) girl, possibly the daughter of a rich, influential white man who had tricked an indigenous woman into sleeping with him. When her mother died, this girl vowed to avenge her by targeting humans, particularly men, who defiled beauty and innocence, especially in nature.

In another story, she was a little girl who became lost in the forest and died before her parents could find her.

She takes her role as the guardian of nature very seriously. If she comes across anyone vandalizing her domain, she will approach slowly, making a quiet, hissing noise before suddenly setting about them, whipping them with her braided hair or stinging vines with unexpected stamina and strength. She can be deterred, like Saci, with gifts. She prefers porridge or honey. She loves to braid and will tightly plait and weave horse tails or lengths of string with astonishing dexterity.

Comadre Fulozinha is a divine entity to the Jurema cult in Paraíba. Though her stories are not as detailed as some of the other entities in the Brazilian myths, her guardianship of nature has made her a popular character and very relevant in the awakened consciousness to preserve the planet.

Chapter Three – River Myths

The mighty Amazon is the centerpiece of the most extensive river system in the world. Other systems in Brazil, such as the Tocantins-Araguaia in the north, the São Francisco in the northeast and east, and the Paraguay-Paraná-Plata in the south, are also significant. The role of these rivers in Brazilian myths is inescapable.

The deity that is responsible for the rivers in the Brazilian pantheon is Iara, the water goddess. She is also known as Yara and Uiara, and she is originally from ancient Tupi mythology.

A mermaid-type spirit, she is usually depicted as half woman, half fish with long hair, sometimes blue or sea green. Her hair is often decorated with red flowers.

In some stories, she was born human. As a girl, she was a skilled, fearless warrior. She had two brothers who were jealous of her natural flair for combat and knew she was far more capable than they were. When she excelled at these things, they were made to look weak and ineffective. They grew to hate her and, in time, resolved to kill her. Knowing she could easily defend herself, they attacked her when she was alone and asleep.

Despite being ambushed in this way, Iara fought back until her two brothers were left slain on the ground. Perhaps she was dreaming that she was in an epic fight.

Iara's father was full of rage when he saw his sons were dead. Without pausing to hear what had happened and mad with grief, he had Iara bound and thrown into the confluence of the rivers Negro and Solimões.

Turning his back on his daughter, he left her to drown.

The Tupi moon goddess, Jaci, had seen what had happened. She knew Iara was blameless. She elevated the girl's spirit and made her into the river goddess.

Here, her story becomes conflated with the European traditions of mermaids and sirens. She was no longer revered for her skills as a warrior. Her beauty and wonderful singing tend to define her. It is said men are driven insane by the sweetness of her voice.

In chronicles published by Portuguese colonists in the 16th century, there is mention of a horrible river monster called the Ipupiara. Its female form is a possible ringer for Iara, as she is described as very beautiful and has some elements of a human woman, including long, flowing hair.

The male Ipupiara is a different matter altogether. Pero de Magalhães Gândavo wrote in his 1564 account about a young indigenous woman who had been enslaved by the colonists. She was named Irecê. She had arranged to meet her lover on a São Vicente beach, only to find he had been brutally mauled by an Ipupiara monster. When she fled in horror and reported what had happened, a Portuguese captain found it and killed it with his sword.

This awful creature was described as being "fifteen hands" (3.3 meters) and "strewn with hair all over its body ... (and) on its snout it had very large silks like moustaches."

The Jesuit priest Fernão Cardim reported even more alarming details. He declared the Ipupiara was "repulsive" and said it killed humans by hugging them tightly and kissing them until they could no longer breathe, smothering them to death. It ate its victims, devouring their eyes, noses, fingertips, toes, and genitals. It was, Fernão Cardim said, "a bestial, hungry, disgusting being, of primitive and brutal ferocity." Historians generally assume that these early colonizers were waxing lyrical about some particularly aggressive form of sea lion or manatee.

Iara often appears in the story of Ruiva ("Red Beard") as a benevolent spirit for good. Long ago, in the state of Piauí in the northeastern region of Brazil, there was a young woman who found herself pregnant after her lover had died. She did not dare tell her family. When the time came for her baby to be born, she slipped away into the forest and gave birth to a son.

Afraid of what her mother and sisters would say, she put him in a copper pot and set him adrift in the river. As she left, a water spirit, often said to be Iara, resolved to save this baby boy, who came to be known as Ruiva. In the process of rescuing the baby, that area of the river became enchanted, which is how the Parnaguá lagoon came to be.

From then on, Ruiva would occasionally appear on the riverbank. In the morning, he seemed to be a baby, and passersby were alerted to his presence by his cries. However, by midday, he would be an amorous adult man with a red beard, desperate to steal a kiss from any young lady he might come across. By evening, he would be a wizened old man.

Another water spirit, Caboclo d'Água ("hillbilly from the waters"), is a creature that resembles a man who harasses fishermen and sailors on the São Francisco River. He forces boats to capsize, releases fish from nets, and even drowns unfortunates swimming in the river.

Caboclo d'Água is often described as a sort of merman with a copper-colored scaly fishtail. His hands are webbed like a frog's, and sometimes, he has a single eye in the center of his forehead.

Sailors and fishermen believed they could avoid his attention by painting a white star on the bottom of their boats or by decorating the bow with a carved carranca figurehead. A carranca could be a human or an animal, but it typically had a wide open mouth and fangs. It was thought the carranca would repel evil spirits from the water.

Some people prefer to try and curry favor with Caboclo d'Água by offering him tobacco or alcohol. If he accepts the gift, he might treat the giver with respect and even guide them toward waters with plenty of fish.

One of the most delightful creatures found only in the Amazon River is the pink dolphin known as the *boto* or *bufeo*. They are found in the basins of the Amazon and Orinoco across South America. It is the largest species of river dolphin; some males grow up to nine feet in length. They are born grey, and as they mature, they become glorious shades of pink, from a pale blush rose to a vibrant shade of bubblegum. Some remain grey with the merest hint of the famous pink, and some develop spots of pink that cover their bodies. It is still not certain why and how they develop in this way. It is possible that their diet, which is rich in shellfish, could play a role. Or perhaps it is a reaction to the sunlight or exposure to the sun. It seems their blood capillaries are nearer to the surface of their skins than in other dolphins, and this may make them appear pinker when aroused or threatened.

Despite their obvious similarities with sea dolphins, the boto has a very different psyche. It is just as agile, but it does not follow boats or jump out of the water. It generally manages to curb its natural curiosity in the presence of humankind. It lives in quiet, small family groups or with its mate and tends to prefer the calmer waters of the Amazon lagoons or flooded areas of the rainforest to stretches of the fast-flowing, open river.

The people who live alongside the Amazon have had a long and complicated relationship with the boto. Their strangeness and ethereal quality have given rise to stories and superstitions that they are protected by some mystical powers, and it is generally accepted that it is bad luck to kill a boto and even worse luck to eat its meat. Naturalists eager to see the rare Amazonian manatee were often advised to befriend a boto since they were considered the elusive creature's guardian.

Fishermen on the Amazon in areas frequented by botos view them with some suspicion. Although some believe they are friends that will lead them to waters full of fish, the botos are also known for luring humans out into dangerous waters, where they quickly find themselves lost. It is said that some even deliberately sink fishing boats so that the fishermen drown.

Some cultures believe the pink dolphin was originally a warrior who was so successful that the world spirits put him under an enchantment before he threatened the very nature of the world. The most well-known and enduring story is that of Boto Cor-de-Rosa, a shapeshifting pink dolphin that appears during summer feasts and celebrations as a sharply dressed stranger.

One version of this myth tells the story of a young woman named Rosita. She was a charming, happy girl who was beloved by all her family. She loved to help her mother with the household chores and often went to collect water from the nearby river.

One warm day, the river sparkled invitingly, and she could not resist taking a swim. As she glided through the cool water, she noticed a young man sitting on the riverbank close to where she had left her clothes. When she finished her swim, she spoke to him. He told her he was a fisherman, and Rosita couldn't help noticing how attractive he was. She arranged to meet him the following day, and after they had met a number of times, she fell in love and spent the night with him.

Rosita's parents began to worry about her. She was spending so much time at the river. When they confronted her, she told them all about her mysterious fisherman and said she wanted to marry him.

Trusting his beloved daughter's judgment, Rosita's father invited the fisherman to the family home and welcomed him with open arms as they arranged for the wedding. The young man was a charming guest, and the family soon grew to love him. However, they couldn't help but wonder why he left each morning without fail and was not seen again until he returned in the evening.

One night, the family had a celebration with a large meal and plenty to drink. Everyone slept well. As the family began to rise, they were alarmed by a shrill screaming coming from Rosita's room. Her father picked up his gun and ran to see what could have happened.

There, beside Rosita on her bed, lay a huge pink dolphin. It tried to wriggle free and head toward the door, but her father raised his gun and shot it dead.

The young fisherman never returned, and Rosita soon found she was expecting a baby. Months later, she died in childbirth. Her baby? It was a pink dolphin calf.

There are many stories of boto men as seductive, feckless lovers who leave young women pregnant and abandoned. In these accounts, the boto is universally dressed in a sharp white suit and, most importantly, a hat. This covers their blowholes, which would give away their true identities. Sometimes, the hat is a shapeshifted (or modified) stingray. Many of the boto man's accessories come from river creatures. For instance, he might wield an electric eel sword or wear catfish shoes. In its creature form, an enchanted boto with the ability to shapeshift can sometimes be spotted by its fin tips that look a little bit like human hands.

At odds with the solitary and quiet demeanor of the boto, once these entities have shapeshifted, they are the life and soul of the party. In one Amazon town, two men with hats enjoyed an evening of hard drinking and a great deal of raucous laughter. At dawn, they were seen leaving town, arm in arm, singing at the top of their voices and carrying bottles. The next day, fishermen caught two botos. While gutting them, the men were overcome by the stench of liquor that emanated from the dolphins' stomachs.

In another account, a sharp-dressed man, complete with a hat, was pestering young women with such persistence that the men of the village felt compelled to see him off. As their cries grew louder, a crowd joined in the chase. As he ran toward the river, three harpoon shots were fired at him. A dead boto washed up on shore shortly afterward with three harpoon darts embedded in its hide.

Some boto men are not quite the love 'em and leave 'em Lotharios. They prefer to lure young women to an underwater kingdom known as Encante. Once the young woman has entered its gates, she can never leave.

These myths were often used to explain unmarried women's pregnancies or pregnancies stemming from incest, prostitution, and rape. The white suit and accessories associated with the shapeshifting boto have some similarities to the white Europeans. Since the colonists violently subjugated the indigenous people, at times killing, raping, and traumatizing the women, it is possible that the boto has borne the brunt, in an allegorical fashion, of some of the most horrible experiences certain Amazon people groups suffered.

Chapter Four – Jaguar Tales

The jaguar, the third largest cat in the world, is native to South America, with half of its population in Brazil. These magnificent creatures are formidable hunters. They will prey on almost any animal they come across. Their strong jaws and sharp teeth can even penetrate hard crocodile skin or turtle shells.

Adult jaguars are solitary creatures that require large territories. They are confident swimmers and the epitome of power and grace. As a result, they have long been regarded with awe and respect by the people who live in the rainforest regions, and they have taken an integral role in Brazilian mythology.

Onça-Boi is the man-eating jaguar that is part of the oral traditions of Amazonas, especially Acre. He is closely connected with the spirit world, but in his earthly form, he can easily be distinguished from regular jaguars by his feet, which are hoofed. He is also said to have horns in some cultures.

Because he has no claws, he cannot climb trees and tends to go hunting with his mate. Then, one of them rests while the other eats, which is markedly different behavior from regular jaguars, which lead solitary lives outside of their breeding seasons. In the stories, people unfortunate enough to encounter the Onça-Boi often make the mistake of climbing a tree, believing they will be safe there. They do not realize that it will wait patiently until its prey is exhausted. When they inevitably fall asleep and tumble from the tree branches, the jaguar creature is waiting below.

The Onça da Mão Torta ("Crooked Hand Jaguar") is a mythical beast that stalks the savanna of Goiás. It has different markings than the big cats native to South America and is striped like a tiger. One of its front paws is twisted and buckled, but this doesn't seem to hinder it from hunting and performing other activities.

He is said to be resistant to gunfire and is the spirit of a nomadic cowboy, much like the myth from the Minas Gerais region of Brazil of a shabby, mysterious cowboy who seems to possess mysterious powers. He is neither young nor old, has a slight build, is relaxed in his demeanor, and rarely speaks. His old horse is thin and as decrepit in appearance as he is. He will unexpectedly appear when there are competitions on farms and ranches, such as ox felling, ring racing, and other races. The other cowboys always defer to his skills and knowledge and are always pleased to see the small figure in his large leather floppy hat that hides his oversized forehead and long beard.

One day, a wealthy farmer in Urucuia was having difficulties rounding up his horses, which were spread out over a huge area. He had the idea of organizing a competition that would be open to anyone who thought they could find his horses and drive them back. He would hold, as was traditional, a great feast for all those intending to compete.

Cowboys and ranchers came from all over arrived. They met at the farm and greeted each other warmly, all eager to prove their worth against each other. But before they could saddle up, a mysterious cowboy was bringing the farmer's horses home. He refused to take any prize or reward and slipped away unnoticed as the party was underway.

The cowboys and herdsmen were not at all surprised, but they could not understand how he managed to do it. Whenever they saw him, he was ambling along on a tired old horse.

Sometime later, farmers began finding their cattle were suffering violent attacks. Something was leaving them dead or gored and torn with horrific injuries. The cowboys gathered to find the cause and try to prevent more valuable cattle from being affected. As they discussed what kind of beast they were dealing with, they realized the mysterious cowboy was not there. They speculated that perhaps he had died or was badly wounded. Perhaps he simply could not be bothered to help. As they spoke, their respect for him gave way to ill will and jealousy.

The next day, they started setting out when the familiar small, shabby figure appeared over the horizon with a herd of wild bulls, the very beasts that had terrorized the cattle. The farmer was delighted, but the gathered men were uneasy and couldn't see how he could have achieved such a feat on his own. They began to suspect he was using witchcraft.

One of the younger cowboys resolved to find out the strange man's secrets and befriended him. The two men rode across the land, rarely speaking, even at the campfires where they cooked simple meals before they slept under the stars.

After the months passed, there was little food available, and the mysterious cowboy's companion began to grow weak from lack of nourishment. One morning, when he struggled to mount his horse, the other man handed him some leaves and told him to wait. He explained that he was going to transform himself into a jaguar to hunt for something they could eat, and as soon as he returned, the young man should stuff the leaves into his mouth. Then, he would return to his human state.

The young man watched him go and wondered whether he had heard correctly in his weakened state. To his surprise, in the bright morning sun, the slight figure of the cowboy seemed to become dappled, and it leaped with all the power and grace of a large cat.

It was not long before a large jaguar returned, snarling, with the hindquarters of some beast in its jaws. It dropped the meat and turned to the young cowboy, but he was terrified. Despite his weakened state, he managed to get on his horse and ride away. He still had the leaves in his hands when he finally came to rest.

As for the mysterious cowboy, he remained a jaguar, roaming the state in search of the young man who knows his secret and can help him become human again.

In other stories, the mysterious cowboy is a shapeshifter who is able to take the form of a jaguar, and some of the problems he was so eager to help with were actually caused by him while in his jaguar state. As he spent more and more time as a big cat, he grew more feline than human. When the ranchers realized that it was him attacking livestock on their farms, hunters in the region resolved to put an end to him. Eventually, they managed to corner him and shot him dead.

In one rather more sentimental version of this story, his young cowboy companion was among the hunters who corned him. As the trapped jaguar saw his traitorous friend amongst his captors, he gave one last moan of sadness—an unmistakably human sound of misery and betrayal—before the bullet was fired. It is said that those who were there could never forget it.

Another jaguar myth from the state of Minas Gerais that is particularly prevalent amongst the Xakriabá people, is Kianumaka-Maña. There are several similarities with the mysterious cowboy myth, but Kianumaka-Maña is no humble cowboy; she is a goddess.

Kianumaka-Maña is a warrior. She is able to harness the strength and cunning of the jaguar. The indigenous people who revered her performed rituals before going into battle in the hope of imbuing her ferocity and fighting skills. She also represents freedom and self-sufficiency and is sometimes depicted as a beautiful woman painted with the markings of the jaguar.

As well as obvious comparisons with the mysterious cowboy, Kianumaka-Maña is a goddess in the tradition of the Greek Artemis and the Roman Diana (goddesses of hunting), the ancient Egyptian lion goddess Sekhmet, and the Norse giantess goddess Skadi that rules over winter and hunting.

In one story, a mother and daughter were out when the mother complained they had little meat to eat recently. The daughter told her she would kill a cow for them, but when she came back, she told her mother to push a branch into her mouth.

The daughter left. Soon afterward, the mother heard the sound of a heifer being attacked by a jaguar. Suddenly, the jaguar leaped toward the mother with its jaws wide open, ready for her to throw the branch between its teeth. However, the mother fled in terror.

The girl never became human again. In the daytime, she hid, and at night, she attacked the farmers' cattle until they begged her to stop, handing her their branding irons as a mark of good faith.

In a related story, a girl named Yndaiá felt bitter and angry about the colonization and invasion of her homeland. In a bid to avenge herself on the cruel Europeans who had settled in the region, she asked a shaman to invoke the spirit of the jaguar and enchant her with it.

Once she was able to shapeshift into the form of a jaguar, she attacked the cattle of these farmers and dragged the meat back to her village, where it could be shared. Whenever she returned, Yndaiá's mother (a much braver woman in this story) would be waiting with a branch to throw into the jaguar's mouth so she could transform into a girl again.

However, one day, the mother was unable to find the particular type of branch required to break the enchantment, so Yndaiá could not shapeshift back into her human form. The worst was to come. The farmers got a posse together to hunt the big cat that had been targeting their livelihoods.

Jaguar-Yndaiá, now the hunted, managed to make her way to a cave and remained there, wondering if her end was near. However, her people had not forgotten her and her generosity and brought her meat. They quietly made their way to the cave and performed rituals and dances all through the night until she became a girl again.

The dreaming tree is another myth with the jaguar at its heart. A young boy, Uaica, lived with his elderly grandfather in a small village. He was not a strong child. The other children were often cruel and made fun of him when he could not join in their games.

One day, these teasing remarks were too much for Uaica. He didn't want to go back to his grandfather, knowing the old man would worry since he loved him so much. Instead, he walked into the forest. He had a great love for nature, and the lush green plants and cool air, perfumed with exotic blooms, made him feel calmer and happier.

Uaica was about to turn back when he stumbled. After climbing to his feet, he saw the most extraordinary sight. Beneath a large tree was a tapir lying alongside a sloth, fast asleep. As he drew closer, as quietly as he dared, he saw there was also an anaconda, a monkey, a caiman, and a mother jaguar with her cubs, all sleeping soundly curled up beside each other.

Uaica suddenly felt weary. He was unable to keep his eyes open, and he joined the animals beneath the tree. As he slept, he dreamed he could hear Sinaa's voice.

Uaica had heard stories of Sinaa since he could remember. He was the magical jaguar man with eyes in the back of his head, and he appeared to be an old man until he bathed. Then, his old skin fell away, and he became a young and handsome man. Sinaa knew all of the secrets of the world, such as where the great forked stick that held up the sky could be found, how to save the world from the perils it faced, and how to heal sick animals and humans.

Sinaa whispered stories to the sleeping boy. Eventually, Uaica awoke. It was dark, and all the sleeping animals had gone.

The next day, Uaica couldn't wait to return to the tree and hear the whispering voice of Sinaa. Again, he found several sleeping animals and curled up with them. The jaguar man continued to tell him his secrets. Day after day, he slept under the tree without eating or running around like the other children. Soon, his grandfather could see that he was wasting away.

Sinaa also began to realize that the boy was sick. As Uaica slept under the tree, Sinaa whispered to him that he had shared his secrets and that he should leave and never come back again.

When Uaica woke, he felt sad. He knew he would miss the jaguar man, whom he had come to love as much as his grandfather, but he had promised that he wouldn't return, and he meant to keep his word.

When he arrived home, he found his grandfather weeping. The old man said it was breaking his heart to see Uaica so pale and frail and begged him to eat. Uaica sat down and shared a meal with him and then told him that he had a secret. After they had eaten, he took his grandfather to the dreaming tree in the forest.

Just as before, there were animals fast asleep around its trunk. As soon as Uaica began to feel drowsy, he told his grandfather that he could go no farther. The old man was curious and drew closer. It did not take too long for him to fall fast asleep between two snoozing peccaries. Uaica watched from a distance.

When Uaica's grandfather awoke, he told him never to tell anyone about the tree; its secrets were too powerful and dangerous for anyone who did not have a pure heart.

As they neared their village, the father of Casimiro, one of the boys who had teased Uaica mercilessly, was weeping. His son had become sick, and the family were preparing for him to die. Uaica asked to see Casimiro. He laid his hands upon the sick boy, and through the healing magic Sinaa had whispered to him, he was healed.

From then on, he and Casimiro became firm friends. There was no more teasing or cruel tricks. Uaica also helped to cure other people who fell sick in his village. He was wise beyond his years, and everyone grew to love and respect this strange young man.

One night, while Uaica was sleeping, the jaguar man visited him again. He told him to build a special house with his grandfather so Sinaa could share more of his secrets with him as he slept. Once the dreaming house had been built, Sinaa told Uaica more secrets about the forest and how to make beautiful things from items he could find there. Guided by his mentor, he collected feathers, flowers, stones, nuts, and shells and created intricate, beautiful jewelry and accessories that everybody wanted.

Although Uaica was happy to teach his creative skills to the other villagers, there was a woman who was particularly envious and resentful of his talent. She resolved to steal the loveliest pieces he had made. She had no idea, however, that Sinaa had taught him how to see everything. Uaica rounded on her. He told her and her friends that because of their greed, they no longer deserved his healing powers.

Then, he vanished, never to be seen again. No one knew what had become of him. Perhaps he was transported to a cave where he could spend the rest of his days dreaming, or maybe he became a spirit so he could join the jaguar man in that strange spirit world beyond the reach of humans.

Chapter Five – Monstrous Beasts

Brazilian folklore has more than its share of monsters, most of which are bloodthirsty maneaters, each with their own individual characteristics.

The Brazilian werewolf, the lobisomem, originates in the Amazon Basin region and is thought to be the product of an incestuous relationship or the offspring of a woman and an ordained priest.

Unlike the European werewolf, which has to wait for a full moon, the lobisomem changes from man to beast if it reaches a crossroads on a Friday night. During Lent, it can transform daily. Once the lobisomem has shed its human form, it rampages the countryside in search of children who have not been baptized. It devours these children with all the savagery of a wild beast.

Earlier accounts of the lobisomem suggest its bestial figure was not always wolfish. Rather, it was a dog, a wild pig, or a cross between the two. He has thick fur, glaring red eyes, and a pungent, rancid odor. Like the wolfman, he walks on his hind legs, but he can run more swiftly than most animals. In his human form, he is a weak individual, sometimes with pointed ears that give away his horrible other life.

The lobisomem can be killed with a thorn from a particular orange plant that has grown on consecrated ground or with a bullet that has been filled with wax from a candle that has been used for three holy Masses. If he is wounded, anyone who touches his blood will be doomed.

The Lobisomem do Acre was reported to have killed calves and a child in Seringal Sardinha in July 1990. Rubber tappers working there ran to the rescue after hearing something savaging the livestock. They said that they came face to face with a lobisomem.

The Gorjala, a monstrous, horrible ogre with one eye, lives on the rocky hills and cliffs of Ceará and Amazonas. He wears body armor made from turtle shells. He is huge and takes long strides that cause tremors. He hunts for humans, which he pops under an arm so he can eat them slowly as he trundles along.

The Labatut, another oversized, man-eating fiend, is best known in the Chapada do Apodi region. He also tends to have one eye like a Cyclops, but he also has thorns, spines, or thick stubby hairs that stick out of his body like a porcupine. He has tusks like a wild pig and runs through small communities at night looking for people to gobble up, preferably children because of their tender meat.

The Labatut is a relatively recent myth based on General Pedro (or Pierre) Labatut, who fought in the Brazilian War of Independence in the 19th century. He was a dreadful character. He was hated by his enemies and his own men for his excessive and needless brutality. Eventually, his army rose up against him. His abject cruelty has led to his reputation living on in Brazilian folklore.

In the northeastern reaches of Brazil, in the Alagoas region, the Pai do Mato is a ghastly giant that terrifies people at night with his maniacal, shrieking laughter that can be heard from miles away. Similar to the other ogres, he is huge, ugly, and hairy. He is supposed to be far taller than the trees in the forests where he dwells, and his footfalls make a booming sound. He can be distinguished (to a degree) by his claws or nails, which are long and sharp. Although he has a taste for human flesh, he tends to stay away from people, but if he is a threat, gunmen are encouraged to aim for his belly button, which is considered to be his weakest point.

The mapinguari, another monstrous creature, was supposed to inhabit the Amazon Rainforest. Its name derives from the Tupi-Guaraní words *mbappé*, *pi*, and *guari*, meaning "a being that has a crooked paw."

According to the story, an ancient shaman discovered the secrets of immortality, which angered the universe since it threatened to unbalance time and existence. Because of this, he was transformed into the horrible mapinguari as punishment and forced to remain in this form for all of eternity.

Descriptions vary, but these creatures are said to be covered in thick, dark, and shaggy fur, which is conveniently bulletproof. The indigenous people from the Tapajós River recount that it can be some three meters tall. Its skin is scaly, and like a caiman, it has large, sharp claws and sometimes just one eye.

Although comparable to a Cyclops, it has been suggested that this entity originated from some unidentified ape or giant ground sloth.

The mapinguari is focused on protecting its fragile environment and is supposed to stalk hunters who venture into the rainforest. When it captures them, it will twist their heads from their bodies before devouring them.

The Brazilian centaur, known as Besta-Fera ("Ferocious Beast"), is another mythical creature that arrived with the Portuguese settlers. He is widely accepted as a representation of the devil or one of his attendants. On the full moon, he may climb out of hell and into the mortal world from the graves of sinners in cemeteries. Once he has shaken himself free, he sets to work, marauding through the streets. When he comes across anyone, he brands them with his mark, and from then on, they are destined to burn in hell.

Some versions have Besta-Fera roaming the forests in search of some pernicious plant with a blood-red flower that is imbued with evil powers. Anyone who crosses his path will be rendered insane.

He is said to have the body of a horse and a human torso, arms, and head. He is accompanied by a pack of wild, snarling dogs, which he whips from time to time. With this same strap, he often metes out lashes to any other people or animals he comes across.

In the northeastern regions of Brazil, Besta-Fera is sometimes used as an insult to describe someone who has been unkind or aggressive.

Boi-Vaquim, a mythological creature from Rio Grande do Sul and the southern states of Brazil, is one of the creatures described by the celebrated poet and historian Contreira Rodrigues (1884–1960). It is a magnificent, mystical bull with golden horns, diamond eyes, and great wings. As it gallops, its horns create sparks of fire.

Unsurprisingly, it is incredibly difficult—perhaps impossible—to rope Boi-Vaquim. Cowboys have been driven mad by their obsession to match their skills against him. Some dread the possibility of an encounter with Boi-Vaquim.

In São Paulo, a different beast marauds the streets at nighttime: Porca dos Sete Leitões ("the Sow with Seven Piglets"). This pig is immense. She snorts and grunts with relish as she determinedly leads her brood that trot along in her wake. She was once, it is said, a baroness who had seven children. She was a proud, cruel woman. When she offended a spirit, she was transformed into her current porcine state. She can only become human again when she finds a magic ring.

In another version, she aborted seven pregnancies, and for doing that, she was made into a monster, with her unborn babies becoming piglets. In another version, the lost babies were due to her violent and cruel husband, and as Porca dos Sete Leitões, she is destined to harass errant husbands, persuading them to return to their families as better men.

In the city of Palmeira dos Índios in Algoas, sometime toward the very end of the 19th century, there lived a rich young woman who was the daughter of a powerful high-ranking officer in the military. She was an unpleasant person. She was self-obsessed and oblivious to the hardships and suffering of others.

This young woman had a pet dog that she adored. She spoiled him with endless treats, and he slept on the softest bed until he died on the same day as the spiritual leader of northeastern Brazil, a priest called Father Cicero. The young woman demanded that her beloved pet should have a full funeral Mass and a wake with a candle and sentinel to guard its soul. This funeral cost far more than most in the city could afford for their own family.

This young woman was at the market buying perfume and frivolous clothes a little while afterward when she came across an old woman who was bowed with grief. She was buying black clothes. The outspoken girl, knowing full well the effect of the loss of the priest upon the community, asked the old woman why she was mourning. When she heard it was for Father Cicero, the young woman laughed and said she would do better grieving for her little dog. However, as the words left her mouth, she snapped at the poor old woman. She fell on all fours and then bounded away like an animal.

By the time she had reached her home, it was hard to see where the woman ended and the dog began. She had cursed herself with her careless words, and her family was compelled to lock her away, fearing the shame she brought upon them. When her parents died, her brother, who felt little sympathy for her, had her locked in a cage, where she remained until the end of her days.

The headless mule is a common theme in Brazilian mythology. The most commonly held belief is that its origins are from medieval Europe, probably Iberia, and the story came to Brazil with the Portuguese colonists in the 16th century.

This Mula Sem Cabeça is generally considered to have been a woman who has been cursed for her sins. The mule varies in its appearance from state to state, but it is generally brown or black with silver or iron hooves that clatter and make an alarming noise. Smoke and flames sometimes billow from its neck where its head should be. Despite having no mouth (although some suggest she does have a head but that it is obscured by fire), it makes a shrill neighing sound or wails and cries like a human woman.

The poor woman who became the Mula Sem Cabeça was either a girl who had sexual relations before her marriage or a woman who entered into a relationship with a priest. For this, she is cursed to gallop over seven parishes, starting and finishing where she committed her sinful act. In some versions of the story, the enchantment ends each morning with the crowing of the rooster. She then returns to her human state, exhausted and naked except for her bridle. At nightfall, she will become a mule and gallop again.

In other versions, she tears through fields and forests, devouring any unfortunate creature in her path. There are several ways to stop her, such as pulling her tack from her, which is no mean feat since it is often said to be red-hot. If it is removed, the curse can be resumed if she is re-bridled.

Failing that, drawing her blood with a needle might stop her, which is somewhat easier than tying her to a cross, which is another cure. Once free of the curse, naked (again), grateful, and faintly smelling of sulfur, she will repent her sins. Tellingly, the priest who broke his vows by entering into this relationship did not suffer any known curses or indignities; the responsibility appears to lay exclusively at his lover's feet.

An unusual mythical being that is said to roam the states of Piauí, Minas Gerais, Mato Grosso, and Rondônia is the pé de garrafa ("Bottle Foot"). He has one leg, and because of this, he is supposed to leave tracks behind him that look like a bottle has been dragged along the ground, similar to footprints left by the giant sloth, which is thought to explain the origin of this entity.

The pé de garrafa is part man with a horn in the center of its forehead. It is covered in hair. It can imitate human voices and lure people deep into the forests, where they quickly become lost. It is not as bloodthirsty as some of the other Brazilian mythological creatures, but it will send people mad with its strange and stupefying gaze.

In the Minas Gerais region, especially in São Paulo, people tell the myth of Corpo Seco ("Dry Body"), a man who was so evil and cruel during his long life that when he died, both the angels and the devil refused to take him. His family buried him, but even the earth refused to accept his body. It laid in its grave, entire and uneaten by worms, never decomposing.

Some claim he was from Monteiro Lobato in Serra da Mantiqueira. He held his parents in a dark cellar and beat them for no reason. He subjected everyone he met to spite and hatred and was killed by a vigilante. The people of Monteiro Lobato loathed him so much that they spat on his grave.

After a long time, he rose from his grave. In the long years that had passed, his hair and nails had grown long, and his body was spindly and emaciated. He crept around at nighttime, hiding and occasionally wailing in self-pity at his predicament. He is sort of like a zombie. He is as evil in death as he is in life, and he kills anyone he comes across by crushing their bodies with his thin, dry arms.

In the state of Piauí in northeastern Brazil, the Cabeça de Cuia ("Gourd Head") is the bizarre specter that protects the rivers Parnaíba and Poty.

The story starts with a young man, Crispim, who lived by the banks of the Parnaíba River with his family. They were poor and relied on the river for food, but it was a hard life. There were periods when there was little fish to be caught, especially during the flood season.

One day, Crispim took the boat out, hoping to catch something for lunch, but there was nothing. Dejected and hungry, he returned home, cursing his bad fortune and his family's lack of funds and food.

His mother, seeing him so despondent, felt sorry for him and went to her neighbor to see if they could offer her something with which to make a meal. All the neighbor had was an ox bone, which they handed to her.

Crispim's mother did her best, but with nothing else available other than a little flour, she could do nothing but boil the bone to make a thin broth. When her son sat down to eat, having spent so many hours fruitlessly trying to fish, he was appalled to be served this bone water. In anger, he seized the bone and threw it at his unfortunate mother, killing her. Crispim did not even try to help her. Instead, he ran away as fast as he could.

As she lay dying, the poor woman cursed her son, and as Crispim ran, his head began to swell and grow until it resembled a large gourd.

No longer human, Cabeça de Cuia (which is what Crispim became) was left to wander Teresina, where the two rivers meet. He desperately wants to atone for his wicked deed and break his enchantment, but to do this, he must devour seven young virgins named Maria, which was the name of his mother.

Driven mad by the curse and in his search for Marias, he frequently and clumsily causes the deaths of bathers and those fishing in the rivers. With his horrible bloated head, he can breathe underwater and swim like a fish. He drags the people he kills to the depths of the rivers.

In a less bloodthirsty version of the myth, rather than being forced to murder and eat seven Marias, he is simply looking for his mother to beg for her forgiveness.

The Capelobo is a mythical beast particularly well known in the Maranhão, Amazonas, and Pará states. It is thought to originate with the indigenous people in those areas. Its name is from the indigenous Brazilian word *cape*, meaning "broken bone," and the Portuguese word *lobo*, which means "wolf," although its etymology is rather more complicated.

The Capelobo is part man but has hooves rather than feet, thick brown hair that entirely covers its body, and the head of a giant anteater. In some stories, its back legs are like those of a goat, and there is also the suggestion that it has some features of a tapir.

Although it generally has the head and mouth of a giant anteater, its diet does not consist of insects. It devours cats, dogs, and sometimes people, squeezing their bodies until they die and then drinking their blood. It also might pierce their skulls to feed on the brains with its long tongue.

The Capelobo lives in the rainforests and roams the wetter regions late at night, hoping to find plump kittens or puppies to feast on. It can be killed but only by a single rifle shot that pierces its belly button, which is a vulnerable part of the body of the more horrible characters in Brazilian mythology.

A common theme in Brazilian mythology is the concept of mystic, floating body parts. A good example of this is the Cabeça Satânica ("Satanic Head"), a bizarre being as vile as its name suggests. It almost certainly originates from Portuguese folklore, with its roots firmly in

Christian hellfire and damnation and designed to keep medieval Europeans in line. It is thought to have gained a foothold in Brazilian lore from colonizers who arrived in the Pernambuco region, but its influence spread throughout the country. It is still feared in some of the more remote areas of Brazil.

Cabeça Satânica is exactly as its name suggests: the disembodied head of a devil that somehow suspends itself in the air late at night. Some of those who recount seeing it explain that it rolls or bounces along the ground before finding an appropriate place to drift in the air. Others say it is carried or led by some kind of specter that melts away when the horrible head finds its prey.

It is usually described as red, sometimes glowing, with a manic grin and, more often than not, long straggling hair (by which its ghost carries it). Its eyes are deathly and unforgettable, and its other features are crude and ugly. It spits fire and has a shrill, cackling laugh.

Of course, as you may expect, it has evil intent. Anyone who touches it or is unlucky enough to have it fall onto them will quickly fall sick and die in a matter of days. In some stories, it can devour people whole. It seems to have no origin story. No one knows who it was or where it came from, and its victims appear to be chosen at random. Those who are unfortunate enough to have an encounter with it are advised to make the sign of the cross or, if they have a straw Palm Sunday cross available, to throw it at him and then quickly run away. These same crosses can be pinned to doors to keep it at bay.

In the state of Pará, there is another floating head, the Cumacanga (or Curacanga), to fear. This head was originally a woman who had an affair with a priest. In other stories, it is the head of the seventh consecutive daughter born in a family. To prevent this fate from befalling a seventh daughter, it became traditional for the sixth daughter to become the baby's godmother.

This head has fiery hair and floats from its body at night, scaring people in the dead of night before returning to its body at the first morning crow of the rooster. If someone sees the disembodied head and offers her a needle, the next day, the (entire) woman is compelled to return it, revealing the identity of the Cumacanga.

The Perna Cabeluda ("Hairy Leg"), another mythical body part with a mind of its own, is a leg covered in thick, dark fur that bounces or hops along the streets in the dead of night when everyone is sleeping. If it comes across a drunkard or an adulterer, it will trip them or give them a sharp kick.

This story began as a joke in the 1970s when a caller to a Recife radio show claimed he had found the leg in his bed, and his wife told him it was an autonomous being that had gotten there by itself. This story seemed to capture the public's imagination, and before long, it became an integral part of Brazilian folklore.

Some claim it was the limb of a wicked man who kicked his mother to death, and others say it was part of a dismembered body that the devil hurled from hell. There is also a rumor that it now has eyes and a mouth on its knee, which suggests the story may continue to develop as the years go by.

Chapter Six – Serpents, Snakes, and Worms

In southern Brazil, a mythical amphibious serpent or worm known as the Minhocão is believed to live or once lived deep beneath the ground and under the water. Described as a huge monster with hard black scales and possibly horns, its body is said to be approximately 20 to 50 meters in length (65 to 165 feet) but could be as long as 80 meters (260 feet). It causes earth tremors and landslides as it burrows underground.

The Minhocão de Pari that marauds the Cuiabá River in the state of Mato Grosso is a well-known example. It was said to attack and eat fishermen on that river when the fish were spawning. At other times, it wallowed in the mud, creating large swampy areas and damaging roads. It even dragged cattle and horses into its lair.

Unlike many of the mythological and legendary creatures of Brazil, there are several documented sightings of the Minhocão and some speculation as to its origins. In the state of Paraná, a young man saw a pine tree suddenly fall to the ground. When he hurried over to investigate, he realized the earth was moving below him, and he caught a glimpse of a massive worm-like creature with two horns driving through the mud. In that same state, a woman walking to a nearby pool for water found the area wrecked and an animal the size of a house crawling away. Some other people arrived too late to see the beast, but they did see the trail its body had left behind.

An engineer named Émile Odebrecht once made a survey of the Santa Catarina uplands. He recorded several deep, irregular, and unexplained trenches that ran alongside a tributary. These were thought to have been caused by the movement of the Minhocão.

In 1849, a description of a dead Minhocão emerged. This account stated the creature's skin was as thick as the bark of a pine tree and had scales like an armadillo. The respected German biologist Fritz Müller theorized that perhaps the Minhocão could be some kind of giant armadillo thought to have been extinct. He also suggested it might be an oversized South American lungfish since it was said to be at its most active during prolonged periods of rain.

The Minhocão is not the only monstrous water snake in Brazilian mythology. The boiúna ("Giant Snake") is a malevolent presence that lurks in the darker corners of the rivers, lakes, and lagoons. This boiúna is a snake so colossally large that the grooves caused by its great undulating body in the shallows are said to have formed the rivers that flow from the Amazon. This snake makes an ominous rumbling sound and has large glowing eyes. Some of the indigenous Amazon people groups believe that it is not a lone spirit; rather, it is the creature that develops from a boa constrictor that continues to grow beyond the approximate eighteen feet (six meters), its maximum length.

The boiúna's shapeshifting ability is not confined to human or animal forms. It is able to assume the shape of a ghostly ship or steamer. When it takes this shape, it cruelly gives hope of rescue to those in peril on the water. With their own canoes capsized or sinking, they swim toward the strange craft promising salvation, little realizing they are hurrying toward their doom.

It also makes direct attacks on humans it encounters on the waters it regards as its territory and drags them down to the depths. There, it gorges upon them in the underwater caves it has dug itself. In a more fanciful story, it takes them to an underwater kingdom for the dead and transforms them into river snakes.

As it swims, the boiúna leaves a telltale V-shaped trail across the water's surface. It is often considered a protector of water life, but its presence in the water is sufficient enough to impregnate women bathing or swimming in those waters.

There is a more sinister and supernatural side to the boiúna. Its luminous eyes give it the ability to mesmerize its victims. It can then steal their shadows, leaving them to die as an *assombrado* ("one without a shadow"), a horrible and miserable demise, as the victim wastes away after a few days.

In the Tocantins River, there was a boiúna called Norato who frequently left the water and disguised himself as a handsome young man. He would dance and party with humans, leaving his snakeskin at the riverbank so it would be ready for his return. This worked well for some time until he carelessly forgot to conceal his skin in his eagerness to dance. A passerby found it. Supposing it might belong to a boiúna, they burned it. Norato returned to the water's edge after a night of high living, but he was unable to find his skin and forced to remain a human.

Unlike some of the monsters in Brazilian myths, the boiúna is considered intelligent. When it has been called upon during a séance, it can divulge a great deal about the underworld, at least according to spiritualists.

Its hypnotic powers can also affect ships, leaving them static and unable to move in remote waters. Many a sailor through the ages have wondered whether mechanical difficulties with their craft may be due to the powers of the boiúna.

The boiúna can be killed or disenchanted. After luring it to the riverbank with a bowl of fresh milk, its throat must be cut swiftly and cleanly, and then its killer must depart quickly without turning back.

The stunningly beautiful Iguazu ("Great Water") Falls are situated on the border between Brazil and Argentina. These are the falls Eleanor Roosevelt famously called "Poor Niagara" when she visited. This waterfall has been sacred to the indigenous Tupi-Guaraní people who lived in the vicinity since ancient times. Some worshiped the snake god M'Boi, who demanded human sacrifices from time to time.

A long time ago, there was a girl named Naipi, a chief's daughter, who was very lovely. Her beauty was such that rivers stopped flowing when she looked at her reflection in their waters. M'Boi demanded that she should be given to him. However, Naipi had already fallen in love with Tarobá, a dashing young man from a neighboring tribe. He had no intention of letting M'Boi have his beloved and arranged to rescue her in his canoe.

The night before the sacrificial ceremony, Naipi fled. They paddled along the river, but M'Boi quickly discovered what had happened. Furious, he began to shift his immense coils. As he moved, the land shifted so that the canoe was forced over the waterfalls. In some stories, the couple is falling for eternity.

In other stories, Naipi was turned into a distinctive central stone for her disobedience and disrespect of the river god. She is destined to be struck by the falling waters forever more. Tarobá became a palm tree on the edge of a cliff where he must watch his lover's torment. He stays there, powerless to help his love. Both are watched over by the vengeful M'Boi from his underwater lair, a cave known as Garganta do Diabo ("Devil's Throat"). Every so often, rainbows form the stretch from Naipi's stone to Tarobá's tree, a manifestation of their love, something that even M'Boi could not destroy.

Boitatá is a fabled land-dwelling snakelike beast that often has similar hypnotic powers to the boiúna. It is rather more ethereal, though, and is often described as a kind of fire snake composed entirely from colorful flames. Sometimes, it can appear as a ball of fire that floats, flies, or suspends itself in the air. It is possible that this myth is strongly influenced by the will-o-the-wisp phenomenon, the pale flames that are naturally produced above marshlands in the evenings.

The snakier version of this entity can breathe fire and is sometimes described as having two horns. It can disguise itself as a burning tree branch and has glowing eyes that blind or unbalance the minds of those who look into them, or it can mesmerize them sufficiently enough to eat their eyes. Anyone unfortunate enough to see the boitatá is warned to remain as still as possible with their eyes closed and to pray for it to pass by quickly.

Paradoxically, this fire snake's purpose is to protect the land from poachers who would set the forests alight. It is meant to frighten loggers who are intent on cutting down trees.

The version of the myth told in Rio Grande do Sul explains how the jungle emerged from the primordial darkness when floods began. Most of the animals ventured onto the higher lands. The Boiguaçu, a snake that lived in a cave, was the only creature able to see in the darkness. It preyed on the animals and ate their eyes until its own glowed and gleamed like two small suns. Its body grew to a great length and then began to burn. The Boiguaçu's body perished as it burned away. All the light from the eyes streamed out of them and created the sun. The boitatá was born at the same time, flying in the jungle skies in a swirl of flames.

In some northeastern regions of Brazil, the boitatá is a catch-all for all of the evil souls that have lived and then died. In the south, the myth has become entangled with the biblical story of Noah and the ark. Here, the snakes that survived the Great Flood, which was said to have freed the earth of wickedness, were punished by fire. Each was filled with flames.

Serpentes de Igreja, "church serpents," are another phenomenon in Brazilian mythology. This is the notion that immense snakes have been sleeping underground for centuries. They must remain undisturbed, or else the religious buildings directly over their heads or the tips of their tails will be destroyed. Sometimes, the entire city will be reduced to rubble.

There are a number of local rituals or processions necessary to keep the snakes sleeping, and these are still performed in São Luis in Maranhão, Lages in Santa Catarina, Itacotiara in Amazonas, Araraquara (this particular serpent is said to be an enchanted child) and Taubaté in São Paulo, and Belém and Óbidos in Pará. In time, however, these efforts will be futile since the snake will awaken when it grows so large that its tail enters its mouth.

The rural area of Santarém at the lower reaches of the Amazon in the state of Pará, northern Brazil, is home to the story of Cobra Honorato (or Norato) and Maria Caninana. The legend takes place in a village near the shores of a river where a young woman found she was expecting a baby. She had not had any sexual relations, but she had bathed in the river. In some versions of the story, she is attacked by the boiúna. When her time came, she gave birth to two black snakes.

Before they could slither away, her old Tapuya midwife baptized them Honorato and Maria. The two women allowed them to go back to the water from where they were descended. The two snakes grew to maturity in the river. The male snake, Cobra Honorato, was good and thoughtful. His half-human parentage enabled him to leave the river at nightfall on occasion and transform into a very handsome young man dressed all in white. On these evenings, he quietly made his way to the home of the old Tapuya woman, his godmother, and ate with her. He treated her with much respect and often stayed with her until it was time for him to slip back into his immense snakeskin and glide back into the waters. His godmother loved him very much.

Cobra Honorato was also sure to help the villagers whenever he could. He fought against predators that might decimate the fish they depended on and, on one occasion, spent three days fighting against catfish in the Trombetas River that had started stealing fish from the Claro River. He saved several people from drowning in the river and rescued damaged boats and canoes.

His sister, Maria Caninana, did not share her brother's personality. She was vicious and aggressive. She liked nothing more than making life unpleasant for the people her brother liked to help. She never visited her godmother. Instead, she preferred to attack solitary figures hunting for shellfish at the waterside and finding sailors clinging onto the wreckage of their boats after being hit by a storm and dragging them down to the bottom of the river.

In the river port of Óbidos in the state of Pará, there is a colossal serpent coiled beneath the municipality, fast asleep. Its head is supposedly beneath the altar dedicated to Santa Anna at Notre Dame, while the end of its tail lays at the bottom of the river. Everyone is aware that should it awaken, the church would collapse, and disaster would befall the people in that region.

Maria Caninana carefully combed the riverbed, searching for the end of the serpent's tail. When she finally found the tail, she bit it hard, hoping to wreak devastation. The serpent stirred, causing a tremor throughout the port, but it did not awaken.

Cobra Norato realized his sister would never stop her campaign to wreak misery on her mother's people, so with a heavy heart, he killed her. After spending some time alone to come to terms with what he had done, Cobra Norato went back to the village. He left his snake skin at the waterside, as he did when he visited his godmother, and found the people were sharing a meal. When they saw him dressed all in white, they made him welcome and asked him to eat with them.

Cobra Norato danced with the girls and chatted with the men. He was respectful to the elderly, and everyone was charmed by this polite, well-mannered young man. When the party came to an end, he disappeared. Just as his new friends realized he had left, they heard the sound of a great snake plunging into the river.

Cobra Norato became a regular visitor to the village. Every year, he pleaded for someone to break the curse so he might remain a handsome young man. He told them that if he was found in his snake form asleep on the riverbank with his mouth wide open, it would take three drops of mother's milk on his tongue and a cut to his head with a blade that had not been used before. His great jaws would snap shut, and after three drops of blood seeped from his head wound, he would walk away from his reptilian remains to enjoy a mortal life. His cast-off skin should then be burned so that no one else might suffer the same terrible enchantment.

Although the villagers felt a great deal of sympathy for Cobra Norato, there were few brave enough to approach him as he slept. His huge, sharp fangs were terrifying to behold. His close friends all carried vials of mother's milk and new blades with them, hoping to help, but they could not force themselves to approach him for the ritual he so craved.

Dejected, Cobra Norato took to swimming farther and farther away from the village, always hoping to meet someone prepared to help him. Eventually, he arrived at the town of Cametá. There, he shed his skin and mixed with the local people. He told them of his plight. A soldier heard him and was determined to help the poor young man.

He took a jar of mother's milk and found Cobra Norato sleeping on the riverbank with his mouth wide open, just as he had said. With no thought for his own safety, the soldier did as the young man had asked. As the blood oozed from his head, the curse was lifted, and Cobra Norato was finally able to start a new life as a human.

Chapter Seven – Brazilian Bogeymen

Brazilian children have been encouraged to behave out of fear of a variety of vile entities, much like the bogeyman. Most of these entities are thought to have been influenced by African traditions, with their stories told by the Black enslaved people brought to South America by the Portuguese colonists. These stories, however, have transformed as they passed through the generations.

Tutu Marambá is one of these horrible creatures. It eats children, and its area of interest is in those kids who won't go to sleep. It is usually described as a formless void of nothingness that hides behind the doors of children's rooms, although some stories say he is an immensely strong and hairy ogre that smells and sounds like a peccary. Another version, prevalent in the state of Bahia that binds these two ideas, sees Tutu Marambá as a shadow creature that is able to transform itself into a wild pig to utilize that creature's speed and strength.

The only known way to protect children from the attention of Tutu Marambá is with songs and lullabies, which are sung softly to an infant at bedtime.

"Bicho Tutu, sai de cima do telhado

Deixa esse menino dormir sossegado!"

"Tutu, get off the roof

Let this boy sleep peacefully!"

However, in the southern regions of Brazil, Tutu Marambá was an ancient warrior. He was a skilled spearman who never failed to fell his target, be it man or beast, and he diligently defended and protected the people of his village. His fame spread with his courageous deeds, and his people enjoyed living in security and treated their champion with gratitude and respect.

But this peace was shattered when an army of foreigners launched an attack. Tutu Marambá was killed by a poisoned dart as he battled to save his village. Sorrowfully, the people mourned him and carried his body to a sacred place where he would be remembered forever. As he was laid to rest, his soul soared away as a beautiful white bird, and this species has come to represent courage and bravery. There is no clear reason why the ancient warrior became a hideous bogeyman, but it is probably due to confusion brought about by their similar names.

The African enslaved people introduced or took on Tutu Marambá as a part of their culture in Brazil. The songs and stories they shared with their children were passed on to their children, and so on. Its name probably derives from the Kimbundu word for "ogre." This language was spoken by those from the Angola region of the African continent.

The indigenous people in the northern regions call this entity Tutu Zambê, a monster with twisted, crooked legs—often crippled—and sometimes headless. This one does not have the patience of the Tutu Marambá. Rather than waiting at doors, it prefers to wander the forests in search of young or vulnerable victims.

Children who cry in the Minas Gerais state of Brazil are at risk of being eaten by the Chibamba, a half-human, half-beast that covers itself with banana leaves. It constantly moves as if it were dancing and is thought to originate from old African stories brought to Brazil by enslaved workers on Portuguese plantations.

Cabra Cabriola is another creature that children feared, but this entity originated from Portuguese folklore. It is a hideous nanny goat with flaming eyes and nostrils that eats naughty boys and girls. It can get into houses by opening doors or climbing in from the rooftops. It is said that when little children cry in their sleep, it is because Cabra Cabriola has taken another victim to feast upon.

Its feet clatter as it runs across the rooftops, and it sings this somewhat manic little song to that rhythm:

"Eu sou a Cabra Cabriola
Que como meninos aos pares
Também comerei a vós
Uns carochinhos de nada!"

"I am Cabra Cabriola
Who eats children in pairs,
And I will eat you too,
A few little oldies!"

Parents in the northwestern states of Sergipe, Bahia, and Alagoas who fear their children are at risk from this monstrous goat advise them to get on their knees and pray. This is their only hope when it approaches their homes.

There is a Brazilian lullaby sung to babies and little ones with an ominous warning:

"Nana neném que a Cuca vem pegar
Papai foi para a roça, mamãe foi trabalhar."

"Baby, that Cuca is coming to get you,
Daddy has gone to the farm, and Mummy has gone to work."

Cuca is a witch in the European tradition that has found its place in Brazilian folklore. She is a horrible, wizened hag set on abducting and harming children. The first Cuca hatched from an egg at the beginning of time, and after a thousand years, she became a songbird renowned for her mournful song. After that, a newly hatched Cuca takes her place.

Unlike her European witchy cousins, Cuca is a spirit that invades the dreams and subconscious, frightening her victims with the most terrifying nightmares. She only sleeps one night every seven years.

Yet another threat to children, this time in the Recife region, is the Palhaço do Coqueiro ("the Clown in the Coconut Tree"), a horrible clown who steals children in order to sell their organs. This is a recent corruption of a mythical clown who was so unsuccessful in his efforts to entertain circus audiences that he ran away. Driven insane by his failure, he climbs into coconut palms to see the moon, which seems to be smiling down at him.

When the moon wanes or on cloudy nights, he climbs down and tries to amuse the people he comes across. If they don't laugh, he flies at them in a rage and often kills them.

Papa-Figo ("Liver Eater") also seeks a supply of children to dismember. He is an elderly man with a long nose and sharp teeth and claws. He carries a large sack on his back in which he puts the bodies of children who tell lies. If he cannot get hold of suitable children, he will take freshly dead bodies from cemeteries.

He is supposed to suffer from some disease, probably the potentially fatal tropical parasitic chagas disease that broke out in the northeast of Brazil. He believes eating the livers of children will help cure him. The usual treatment for those suffering from chagas was a liver puncture.

In the state of Bahia, there is another bogeyman entity, the Quibungo. This truly awful creature, believed to be of the Angola and Congo tradition, is a hybrid of creatures, including an ape, a vicious dog, and sometimes a wild pig. It is distinguishable from other fantastic Brazilian beasts by the second huge mouth on its back, which it uses to devour children whole.

In one commonly held tale, the horrible Quibungo finds a little girl playing outside on her own one evening. He grabbed her in his second mouth and then made off, intending to enjoy eating her at his leisure back in his cave.

The little girl started to sing from inside the Quibungo's mouth, asking her mother to come and save her. Her mother, however, had warned her not to play outside on her own in the dark. Though she heard the sad little song, she refused to help.

The little girl continued to sing, but her other relatives took the same stance as her mother, and no one made any effort to save her until the Quibungo approached the house where the girl's grandmother lived. This old woman quickly filled a pot with boiling water. As he passed, confident that he wouldn't be challenged for his supper, she threw the water over his feet, scalding him.

As the Quibungo fell to his knees in agony, his back mouth opened to howl in pain, and the little girl hopped out. Her grandmother hadn't finished with the child-eating fiend. She stabbed him in the neck with a burning skewer, killing him.

The little girl remained with her grandmother and never played out at night again, as there were plenty more Quibungos willing to snatch a tasty young child.

Cautionary tales are not restricted to bogeymen characters. There are also witch-type characters that are influenced by the European tradition;

these figures likely have their origins in the Portuguese culture that developed in Brazil.

In folklore from the northern regions of Brazil, Matinta Pereira was an old woman with the ability to shapeshift into a bird. In her earliest form, it was said that she could communicate with animals in their own languages and that she had the ability to control the weather and even summon storms. Her story has since developed. Rather than being the wise woman of the forest with musical powers to inspire awe and respect, she became a mean-spirited, more unpleasant character over the centuries.

In her more recent form, she is a witch who can turn herself into a bird, generally thought to be the striped cuckoo, although some say a barn owl. In this form, she flies onto the roofs of houses at night and makes dreadful screeching and squawking noises so that the people inside cannot get any sleep. She only stops this commotion if they offer her a gift—usually coffee or tobacco—and flies away.

The following day, she arrives at the same house, this time in her human form, to collect the promised gift. If it is not forthcoming, she curses them with the promise of disease or death.

This witchy Matinta Pereira is believed to be a hereditary malediction passed from mother to daughter. If there is no heiress to this horrible hex, she can try to pass it on if she can find someone to agree. Vain and greedy women are at particular risk of being tricked into taking this responsibility.

Villages determined to rid themselves of Matinta Pereira have a special ritual. A key must be buried near where she is expected to appear. Scissors are placed over the earth, covering it, along with a rosary (for best results, each bead should be separately blessed). When Matinta Pereira walks over it, her spirit will be trapped, and her curse must be swept away with a broom to ensure it will not fester.

Pisadeira ("Stamping Woman") is another witch-like entity. She is described as a hag with the eyes of the devil. She is best known in the Minas Gerais region, particularly in São Paulo.

She has the horrible, cackling laugh synonymous with witches and has a foul and putrid odor about her. Physically, she has a big nose, a turned-up chin, and a twisted, wide mouth. She can be skinny or fat. She is often depicted with long, bony fingers and is dressed in tatty rags, sometimes with a red cap.

She climbs upon rooftops, searching for greedy people who have gone to bed with full stomachs after eating too much. When she finds one, she climbs onto them so they cannot breathe.

Pisadeira was used to explain the phenomenon of sleep paralysis and has similarities to the concept of the incubus, which is said to cause nightmares and night terrors among Europeans. Pisadeira was the subject of some verses by the celebrated Brazilian poet Cora Coralina (a nom de plume of Anna Lins dos Guimarães Peixoto Bretas). "The Pisadeira comes, won't let you sleep, and in the morning, you are broken like hell."

Folklorists believe Pisadeira might have developed from the Portuguese mythical character Fradinho da Mão Furado. He is a friar who disturbs sleepers. When they awake, he presses his hands on their chests to stop them from screaming.

Chapter Eight – African Influences

In Brazilian mythology, several legends can be traced back to early Portuguese and Moorish stories. For instance, stories of beautiful princesses who are cursed in order to guard treasure hoards and stories of snake princesses have permeated the folklore of northern Brazil.

In the Middle Ages, the North African Muslim people (often referred to as the Moors) were frequently in conflict with the Europeans in the Iberian Peninsula. For seven hundred years, the Arabian and Moorish forces had a presence in the region and were only defeated in Spain as the Age of Exploration began in 1492.

The presence of the Moors made a deep impact on Iberian culture, particularly in literature and architecture, but with their defeat and the creation of the modern countries of Spain and Portugal, the Moors were treated with disdain and enslaved for cheap labor and frequently shipped across the Atlantic to help build the new colonies in South America.

Jericoacoara, in the municipality of Jijoca, Ceará, has a lighthouse. It is said that beneath it, closed off by huge iron gates, lies a wonderful city full of beauty and riches. However, the gates of this city are guarded by a huge serpent with golden scales and the head and feet of a woman, an enchanted princess called Carolina, the *Princesa Encantada de Jericoacoara*.

Her curse can only be lifted after a human sacrifice has been performed immediately outside the city's gates. Some of the blood from that unfortunate has to be painted along her scaly back. Then, she will become the beautiful princess she was, her marvelous city of riches will open, and she will marry her rescuer (who has a questionable character, having just slaughtered an innocent person on a somewhat sketchy premise). This hero will become lord and king of her realm.

Another of these enduring myths that is believed to have its roots in the arrival of the Portuguese colonists is the story of Teiniaguá, another Moorish princess.

The beautiful Teiniaguá managed to escape the brutal attention of her Spanish oppressors and fled to the south of Brazil. There, she encountered Anghangá, who promptly cursed her. She became a salamander with a gleaming ruby on her head. She is destined to remain in a lagoon in the Jarau crater in the Paraná Basin, Rio Grande do Sul.

In the nearby small town of São Tomé, there was a young sacristan who served the priests at the church. He visited the lagoon, and when he saw the salamander, he captured it in a bull horn and took it back to his lodgings at the church.

In another version of Teiniaguá's story, the sacristan was distracted by a bubbling sound that seemed to come from the heart of the lagoon. The noise seemed to become louder and louder until he felt sure the whole lake was being boiled. Then, an unearthly light from beneath the water began to grow brighter and rise in a ball as if to head for him. Terrified, the sacristan tried to flee but found he was unable to move. Suddenly, in a flash, the light transformed into a jeweled salamander with a ruby on its head. The young man quickly captured it in a bull horn and took it back to his lodgings at the church.

He remembered hearing an old story about an enchanted lizard that, if treated well, would guide a good man to a cave full of treasure. He wondered if the tale might be true. He carefully opened the horn, ready to feed the salamander, when there was a blinding flash. A lovely young woman stepped out of the horn and grew larger and larger until it was clear she was human.

The sacristan had never seen such perfection before and wondered whether he had captured a goddess at the lagoon. He fell to his knees in awe, and then, turning to him, she spoke. She told him that she had been cursed by a foul demon and explained that she was an unfortunate princess. When the sacristan tried to apologize for his humble surroundings that ill befitted her beauty and status, she laughed softly. As he looked around, his spartan room had become furnished with the richest, most exotic furnishings. The dark walls now glistened with sparkling light as though they were embedded with gemstones and pearls, and the air was scented with sweet and heady perfume.

Teiniaguá then told the astonished young man that she would be his lover. The two spent the night together in his enchanted room, but in the morning, she disappeared. The poor sacristan was exhausted and devastated. He looked dreadful with his tired, red eyes and found it difficult to concentrate on his work, worrying the priests. They wondered what could be the matter with their young attendant who was usually so diligent.

For his part, the sacristan was concerned about his sins and longed to confess, but he could not bring himself to betray Teiniaguá. That night, when he retired to his room, she returned, and they loved each other again. From then on, she came to him every night.

One evening, Teiniaguá asked the sacristan to let her taste the communion wine. Unable to refuse his beloved, they went to the church and drank chalice after chalice of the sacred wine. After making love by the altar, they fell asleep.

The next morning, the sacristan awoke, but he was not alone. The priests found him surrounded by the trappings of his debauchery, but Teiniaguá, as usual, had disappeared. The townspeople were appalled at his behavior, and since he refused to say who he had been with in the church, he was sentenced to death. The young man was crippled by shame and guilt, but he was even more devastated at the thought of never seeing his princess again.

A crowd gathered to watch his execution. Suddenly, a bolt of lightning came as if from nowhere, and a shining figure rose from the lagoon. Teiniaguá, shimmering in her beauty, appeared before the crowd, who ran away terrified. She turned to the sacristan and led him away to the caves of Cerro do Jarau, where they remained for two hundred years, guarding the fabled treasure there.

However, this enchantment was not permanent. It could be broken if someone completed seven specific trials. When this person was granted a wish, they could ask for the treasure and the couple guarding it to be freed. After two centuries had passed, a man completed these trials but asked for nothing in return. As he left, the sacristan gave the champion a golden coin.

A few days passed, and the man heard that one of his neighbors was selling his herd of cattle, so he went to buy himself a bull. He picked up the golden coin, and to his surprise, it multiplied and continued to multiply until he had enough coins to buy the whole herd.

News quickly spread, and people wondered how this man, who was known to be poor, had managed to afford the cattle. They concluded that he must have made a pact with the devil. They refused to trade with him and ostracized him. Soon, he could bear it no longer and returned the herd to his neighbor in exchange for the enchanted golden coin, which he took back to the cave.

When he gave it back to the sacristan, the curse was broken. Teiniaguá and her sacristan left the cave and settled in Rio Grande do Sul, where the people of Iberian-Amerindian heritage are said to be their descendants.

There are many myths and legends in Brazil's canon that undeniably have their origins in the shameful period of slavery.

São Luis is the capital and largest city of the state of Maranhão, home to the indigenous Tupinambá people. It has an interesting history, particularly since it was founded in 1612 by a French naval officer and then swiped by the Portuguese three years later. It was also under Dutch occupation between 1641 and 1644. In recent times, it has become the heart of reggae in Brazil and has a vibrant and popular culture.

São Luis is also home to the ghostly story of Ana Jansen's carriage. In the dead of night, an antiquated rattling carriage hurtles through the streets. It is pulled by headless horses and guided by a coachman, who also is missing a head. If that wasn't enough, the clatter of the carriage is accompanied by wails of tormented souls or the squealing of gears in need of oiling.

Inside the carriage is the heavily veiled Ana Jansen, whom no one has quite managed to see. In life, she was said to be an evil slave owner who meted out cruel punishments for no reason at all. Her haunting is an attempt to atone for her wickedness, as she implores passersby to pray for her soul from inside her darkened carriage.

Ana Jansen was a real person. In the 19th century, she was banished from the family home when it was discovered she was pregnant. She then had a love affair with Colonel Isidoro Pereira, the wealthiest man in the province. He had made a fortune from his cotton and sugar plantations, where enslaved African workers provided the heavy labor.

When he died, Ana Jansen took over his business interests and was very successful, so much so that Dom Pedro II, Emperor of Brazil, called her the "Queen of Maranhão." Though it is certainly true that she had more enslaved workers than anyone else in the region, there is no tangible evidence that she was any crueler than any other slave owner.

Even in her lifetime, there were rumors of her cruelty and wickedness. She was said to have had numerous affairs with prominent figures to increase her wealth and status. She was supposed to have poisoned the town's water supply by throwing dead cats in the wells so that the townspeople were forced to buy water from her.

Her supposed treatment of slaves was incredibly brutal. She would have them prostrate themselves face down on the ground so she could walk on them to save her shoes from getting muddy in rainy weather. Any enslaved person she considered disobedient or too pretty would be flung into a pit of spikes. It was said the people of Maranhão hated her. A merchant saw this as a business opportunity. He ordered a large number of *penicos* (a chamber pot) bearing an image of her face at the bottom. Ana Jansen heard about this and quietly sent her staff to buy all of them. Days later, this merchant opened his front door to find every *penico* had been left there. They were full of human excrement.

There seems to be little doubt that her reputation was embellished or even completely made up. This myth serves as a good example of women being vilified for their successes.

There is a legend about the procession of the dead that shares elements of Ana Jansen's story. It concerns a nosey old woman who spent her time at her window spying on her neighbors for anything she could gossip about. She was well known for her uncharitable behavior and spiteful ways.

One Ash Wednesday, late at night, she was at her window, as usual, when she saw a procession of hooded figures slowly making their way through the street. She knew the church had not planned any such procession, and in any case, it was far too late for such activities. Despite this, she remained glued to the window, desperate to know what was going on.

As the figures passed her home, one of the figures handed her a candle, and then they were gone. With no more to see, the old woman went to bed, but the next morning, she went to pick up the candle, only to find it was a human bone. Needless to say, she realized the folly of her ways and never snooped or gossiped again.

Some believe this procession of spirits that walk at midnight are the spirits of the African people brought to South America by the Europeans who never saw their families or homelands again. Because of this, their lives are unfinished, and they need to march to get some kind of closure before their souls can move on to the next world.

The procession is also thought to be a portent of death. The leader of the ghostly marchers is said to knock on the door of the next person in the community who will die.

In the tradition of haunted floating body parts that pervade Brazilian mythology, there is a disembodied hand with black hairy skin. This mythical presence is believed to materialize mostly in the southeastern regions of Brazil and is especially prevalent in São Paulo. It is known as Mãozinha-Preta ("Little Black Hand") or Mãozinha-da-Justiça ("Little Hand of Justice"), and it is thought to be the spirit of an African enslaved person brought to Brazil.

Its reason for existence is to help protect African Brazilians from racist attacks and to mete out justice if any of them are hurt. It will pinch, slap, or strike anyone it perceives to be a threat to those it protects.

In the age of slavery, exhausted Black laborers could call on the hand for help when they were overwhelmed by work, knowing it would never harm them. In one story, a greedy slave owner called upon it to do the work of some of his workers, and it reluctantly agreed. But when the slave owner ordered it to beat his slaves, it turned on him in anger and beat him within an inch of his life. He was lucky; some say Mãozinha-Preta will strangle its enemies.

Chapter Nine – Folktales and Fairytales

The Brazilian story of Domingo's cat has strong similarities to the European Puss in Boots, Dick Whittington, and Aladdin from the *Arabian Nights*.

Domingo was a young man who had a cat that he adored. He was poor and would gladly sacrifice his own needs to ensure his cat was fed.

One day, his cat told him not to worry anymore because he was taking control and would make their fortune. He went into the forest and dug a hole. He found five pieces of silver. He bought some food for himself and Domingo and then took the rest of the silver to the king.

The next day, the cat went back to the forest and dug up several pieces of gold, which he took to the king as well. On the third day, he dug up diamonds and gifted them to the king.

By then, the king had started to ask who was giving him these fine gifts, and the cat was presented to him. The cat told him that they were from his master, Domingo.

The king thought that this Domingo must be extremely wealthy and a potential husband for his lovely daughter. He asked the cat to bring Domingo to the palace so they could arrange a marriage.

When the cat told Domingo, he protested that he couldn't possibly marry the princess. What could he possibly wear? The cat told him not to worry, and he returned to the royal palace. He told the king that there had been a terrible fire where Domingo's clothes were made and kept, and his tailors had burned to death. He asked the king if Domingo could borrow something suitable. The king, sympathetic in the face of this calamity, loaned Domingo one of his finest costumes.

Domingo put it on and looked just like a noble prince, but he was still concerned. Where would he and the princess live?

The cat told him not to worry and traveled through the forest to a mountain where a giant lived in a palace. The cat politely asked the giant to loan this fine palace to his master, but the giant was outraged at the request and refused. The cat promptly turned the giant into a mouse and then killed and ate him.

Domingo and the princess were married and sailed down the river on a magnificent barge to the giant's palace. It was filled with riches beyond their wildest dreams. Domingo turned to his cat to thank him for all he had done, but he had gone.

The mysterious, clever, and wise cat had gone to bring good fortune to someone else who valued him beyond all else. Domingo never forgot him, and he lived a long and happy life with his princess.

In a story that explains how pigeons became tame, a father had three sons ready to leave home and make their way in the world. He gave each of them a large melon with the warning only to open them by water.

In fairytale tradition, the brothers each took a different path. It was a hot day, and the eldest opened his melon as soon as he had left so he wouldn't have to carry it. To his amazement, a beautiful young woman stepped out of the fruit and asked him for water or milk. The young man had neither, and she fell to her knees and died.

The second son had chosen a path that took him uphill. He quickly became hot and tired. He soon became unbearably thirsty and broke his melon, eager for some of the juice inside. Just as before, another lovely maiden stepped out of it, asking for water or milk. He, too, was unable to provide either, and she died there and then.

The third brother was finding his journey just as difficult. The terrain was difficult, and he grew tired and thirsty, but he did not forget his father's advice. He continued to carry the heavy, cumbersome fruit.

Eventually, he reached a town where he saw a fountain. After taking a drink himself, he opened his melon, and a beautiful woman stepped out. As soon as she asked, he gave her some water, and then she hid in a nearby tree while he went to find some food for them.

As she waited, she watched the townspeople coming to the fountain for their water. A pretty little enslaved Black girl carrying a large pot on her head couldn't resist admiring her reflection in the water. As she gazed upon her own face, she thought to herself that she shouldn't be carrying water for her lazy old mistress and threw the pot to the ground, smashing it into thousands of pieces.

However, when she returned without the pot or water, she was whipped as a punishment and sent out again with a new water jar. As she bent to fill it, she heard the young woman in the tree laughing softly. Realizing that her moment of vanity must have been seen by someone, she angrily took a pin from her pinafore and plunged it into the woman in the tree. When its sharp point pierced her skin, she transformed into a pigeon.

The young man returned, and the Black maid, terrified, hid herself in the branches of the tree. When he saw her, he couldn't understand what had happened, but the little maid quickly told him that she had been badly sunburned while she had waited for him. Satisfied, he took her with him, and they got married.

However, the young man always felt uneasy about his bride, and her sunburn never faded. Over the years, he became very wealthy, and he bought a grand house for his family, with a magnificent garden that became his pride and joy. He delighted in the exotic, perfumed plants he could grow, and birds came from far and wide to sing in this special place. As the man sauntered along his garden paths, a pigeon always seemed to follow him. The bird constantly flew around him, which he found very irritating.

When his wife fell sick, he ordered that this pigeon should be cooked for her. As it was being roasted, the cook noticed something was embedded in the bird's breast. None of the kitchen staff could pull it out. She called to the master, and he was easily able to pull the pin from the pigeon. Instantly, it transformed into the lovely maiden who had come from the melon.

Faced with this woman, the man's wife wept as she admitted what she had done and then (conveniently) died. The melon woman and the man married and had a long and happy life, but she always remembered her life as a pigeon. Until then, these birds had always lived deep in the forests and away from the towns. She had little houses built in the garden so that they could nest there. In time, families of pigeons saw the houses and nested in them, laying their eggs and raising their chicks in that beautiful greenery.

From then on, pigeons (according to the story) became accustomed to living alongside people and left the forests to nest in the cities of Brazil.

The manioca, or cassava plant, is a woody shrub native to South America. Its starchy root is one of the pillars of Brazilian cuisine and can be used in several different ways. It can be used much like a potato, it can be dried and ground into flour, and it has proven health benefits.

The myth of how it came to be has been passed down through the generations. Once upon a time, the daughter of an important chief found she was pregnant. She had never had a relationship before and could not explain how it had happened, but her father did not believe her. He punished her cruelly, demanding to know the identity of her baby's father. However, she couldn't tell him; she truly had no idea how it had happened.

After nine months had passed, she gave birth to the most astonishing child. This little girl, named Mani, could walk and talk before she was a year old. Her sunny disposition endeared her to everyone.

Then, suddenly, with no explanation, Mani died. The community was distraught, and the chief of the village insisted that she should be buried in his home near where he slept.

Soon afterward, a strange plant began to grow from her grave, and a spirit came to the chief in his dreams. It told him to dig up the plant for the root, which would bring sustenance and good health to his people. He did this, and the cassava has since become a staple in people's diets.

There are several stories about the animals of the jungle. Many are in the tradition of explaining why they have certain characteristics, such as why the toad has bruised skin and how the rabbit lost its tail. Monkeys have more than their fair share of these folktales. The most well known of these monkey tales explains why they believe bananas belong to them.

An old woman had a marvelous garden in which she grew bananas that were the envy of everyone who saw them. Because she was old and not strong or agile enough to climb up the trees to harvest the fruit, she asked the biggest monkey to do it in return for half of what she had grown.

This monkey set to work and did as he had been asked. However, when he finished, he took all the ripe large bananas as his half and left the old woman with the smaller, tougher fruit that grew at the bottom of the trees.

The old woman was furious that she had been tricked and resolved to get her revenge on the big monkey. After a great deal of thought, she made a little boy from wax and put a basket on top of his head so he looked just like a peddler. Then, she found the plumpest, sweetest, and yellowest bananas and arranged them in the basket.

Soon enough, the big monkey passed the little wax boy and saw the tempting bananas. In his most wheedling, pitiful voice, the monkey begged the boy for a banana. Of course, the wax boy said nothing.

The big monkey wasn't used to being ignored and angrily said he would push him if he wouldn't give him a banana. Still, the wax boy stayed silent, so the big monkey gave him a sharp push with his right forepaw.

His paw sank into the wax and stuck firm. The monkey was furious and demanded the wax boy release him immediately and give him two bananas. Otherwise, he would push him again. The boy gave no response, so the monkey pushed him again.

With both forepaws stuck in the wax, the big monkey was burning with rage and kicked the boy so that his hind paws were also stuck. He roared and howled until almost every monkey in the forest came to see what terrible calamity had befallen the biggest monkey.

The littlest monkey had the idea that they should all climb on top of each other into a huge pyramid, with the loudest monkey at the top, so he could call out to the sun and ask for help.

The sun was sympathetic to the biggest monkey's plight and sent its hottest rays to melt the wax until the biggest monkey could pull his paws free.

The poor old woman was aghast to see the sun helping the monkeys. They laughed, cheered, and made rude gestures at her. She could see there was no point in her continuing to remain there. She left her banana garden to the jubilant monkeys and moved a long way away. She grew cabbages in her new home.

The colorful wing cases of the beetles of Brazil are explained in a fable similar to Aesop's tale of the tortoise and the hare. It begins at the time when all beetles were brown. A grey rat saw a little female brown beetle making slow but steady progress as it walked along a wall. The rat mocked it for its lack of speed.

The rat showed her how fast it could dart and scurry, but she barely looked, instead continuing on her way. A blue and gold parrot that had been watching with interest from its perch flew down and suggested that if they raced, it would provide a new coat in whatever bright colors the winner wanted, courtesy of its friend, the tailor bird.

The drab little beetle and the dull grey rat found this prospect irresistible. Both dreamed of a glow-up. The rat boasted that he would soon have orange stripes like a tiger, as he was certain he would win.

When the race began, the little beetle started determinedly. The rat saw the laborious progress she was making and saw no point in rushing, but when he reached the finish line, the little beetle was waiting there for him. "How could this be?" he wondered.

The little beetle explained that she had decided to fly. The rat hadn't realized that she had wings and accepted he had been beaten. The parrot was as good as its word, and the little beetle was given a beautiful coat of green that sparkled with gold in the sunlight.

For a long time, beetles were delighted with these green coats until, one day, another little beetle longed to be as blue as the summer sky. She went to the tailor bird and begged him to make her an azure coat.

The tailor bird agreed but told her she would have to lose something. The little beetle agreed readily. When the coat was made, it was even more beautiful than the little beetle had imagined, with gleaming silver sparkles. She put it on and quickly realized what she had lost. It was soft rather than lacquer-hard like her green and gold coat had been, and from then on, she never grew again. This is why the blue beetles of Brazil are much smaller than their cousins.

This story finishes with the Brazilian flag. It is suggested that the background is the emerald green of the first beetle's coat, and the yellow diamond is its golden sheen. Within that is a blue circle that represents the earth. It is thought this represents the smaller beetles, and the white stars are just like the silver sparkles that enhance its coat. Underneath is Brazil's motto, "Ordem e Progresso" ("Order and Progress"), words that the wise little beetle might have called out when she raced the rat.

Conclusion

Despite the varied and extraordinary creation myths handed down through the generations, there is a notable lack of eschatological myths unique to Brazil that have survived, assuming they ever existed. There is, of course, the Armageddon and Day of Judgment in the Christian tradition. Catholicism is still the most widely practiced religion in Brazil (in 2020, 54.2 percent of the population identified as Catholic).

This lack of concern about the end of days is probably due to the fundamental belief in renewal and regeneration and a strong sense of spirituality. Death is accepted as a part of existence in most of the indigenous belief systems, but through social and sexual reproduction, it is accepted that society will continue and evolve as it always has. Remembering ancestors and heritage is important, and shared community stories help to fulfill this need. Beyond death, the spirit worlds are vague and beyond the grasp of humans (although some shamans are thought to be closer to understanding these secrets), and this belief has served to help build a strong and secure society with shared values and cultures.

The mythology of Brazil gives us an insight into the beliefs, values, and cultures of societies that once existed and continue to develop in this large, diverse part of South America. These stories teach life lessons that are often still relevant today.

Through the centuries, those people who have lived in Brazil celebrated their ancestors and reared their children in the same traditions, demonstrating a better understanding and respect for their environment. They were far better able to balance their existence than later, more sophisticated cultures that invaded and colonized with little regard for the future and the earth.

It is noticeable that many of these stories are concerned with protecting the natural world and punishing those who seek to destroy it. Mãe do Ouro ("Gold Mother"), for example, is an entity devoted to stopping the destruction of the landscape for that most desirable of natural elements, gold. Her presence has been recorded in the gold-rich states in the southeastern, northeastern, and central western regions of Brazil since the gold rushes of the 18th century, particularly in Mato Grosso, Goiás, and Minas Gerais. She is powerful and determined, ensuring those searching for gold cannot exploit the country's mines. Some say that anyone who rests their eyes on her will not live to tell the tale.

There are a lot of details about her appearance. She is beautiful and very fair, and she wears a long white gown that reflects the sunshine, giving her an aura of gleaming brightness. She can transform into a fireball when the need arises.

Her presence indicates that there are gold deposits nearby, and some gold prospectors believe she might lead them there if she believes they can be trusted to take just enough for their personal fortunes and promise never to reveal the location to anyone else.

Sometimes, Mão do Ouro is considered a guardian of wronged women, those beaten or abused by their husbands and living in misery. She is thought to lure these unpleasant men to a cave far from their homes, and there they remain for the rest of their lives while she finds good men who will treat their widows with decency and respect.

The beautiful archipelago of Fernando de Noronha, which lies off the northeastern coast of Brazil, is made up of twenty-one islands as a part of the State of Pernambuco. It is a major tourist destination and a UNESCO World Heritage Site. Its history is turbulent and fascinating. It has always had a limited population; in fact, it has been uninhabited at times and was a jail for Brazil's most dangerous criminals for long periods in the 18th, 19th, and 20th centuries.

These islands have several of their own myths and folktales that demonstrate the range and depth of Brazilian mythology and how these stories have been shaped by history. For example, there is a phantom gypsy woman who offers visitors cashew nuts. Her origin story is tied to the compulsory deportation of Romani people to Fernando de Noronha in 1739.

Another entity firmly linked to the islands' history is the headless priest who rides his white mule across the spectacular sun-bleached beaches at Quixaba. This is thought to be the spirit of Francisco Adelino de Brito Dantas, who discovered a source of drinking water for the grateful islanders. It is not certain why he lost his head and rides across the bay in death.

The spirit of a woman who was betrayed by her husband is said to live inside Morro do Pico, a mountain in Fernando de Noronha. A ravine will appear, in which a door will open, revealing a bright light. The spirit, in the form of a lovely woman, exits the door to find a young man to bring to the mountain with her. He will never be seen again, though his faint screams can be heard for several days.

Alamoa, who was once queen of the archipelago, is another seductress. She is unhappy with the islands being inhabited. She wanders as a stunning young woman around her former kingdom, looking for men to ensnare. Once she has their attention, they are lost. She either takes them to the top of Morro do Pico, where they feel compelled to jump to their deaths, or she traps them in her cave. Once there, she returns to her natural state—a rotting skeleton—and the men die of fright.

Unlike the other female spirit of the mountain, she cannot bear light. Some of the prisoners held in the island jail recounted how they would see her before a storm. She seemed to be dancing, suspended in the night air, and completely naked.

Her name is thought to come from the Portuguese *alemã*, meaning "German woman," and she is supposed to be blonde and blue-eyed with very fair skin. However, it is more likely that she was originally a character from a Dutch tale. They briefly occupied northeastern Brazil in the 1600s.

These stories serve as a microcosm of Brazilian mythology. These tales take elements from the oral traditions of the indigenous tribes, details from real events, and moral or cautionary messages. They blend the natural world with the spiritual world, showing the importance of both worlds in everyday life.

If you enjoyed this book, a review on Amazon would be greatly appreciated because it would mean a lot to hear from you.

To leave a review:
1. Open your camera app.
2. Point your mobile device at the QR code.
3. The review page will appear in your web browser.

Thanks for your support!

Here's another book by Enthralling History that you might like

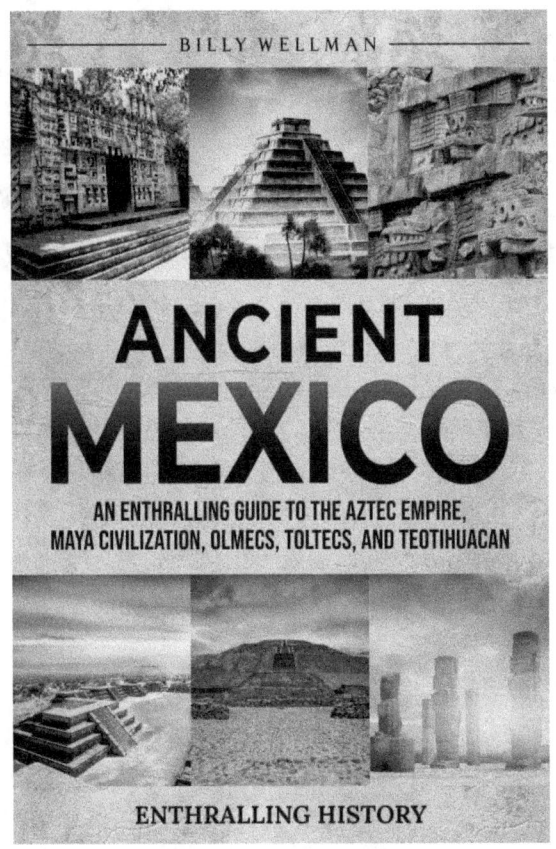

Free limited time bonus

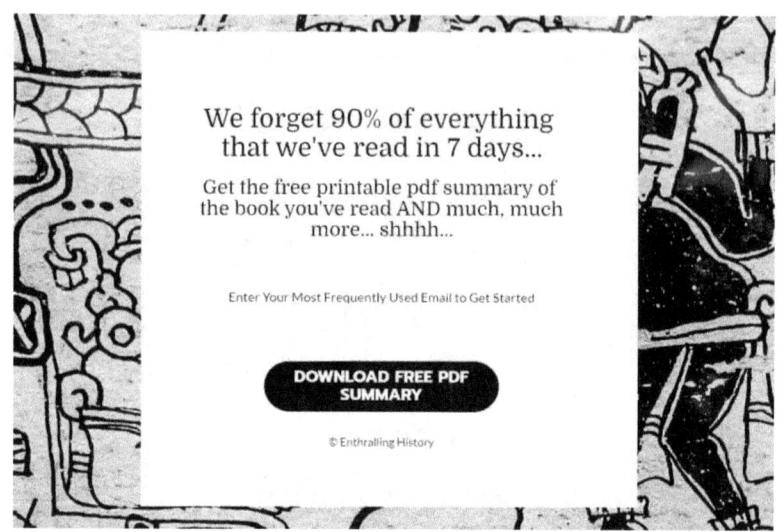

Stop for a moment. We have a free bonus set up for you. The problem is this: we forget 90% of everything that we read after 7 days. Crazy fact, right? Here's the solution: we've created a printable, 1-page pdf summary for this book that you're reading now. All you have to do to get your free pdf summary is to go to the following website:

https://livetolearn.lpages.co/enthrallinghistory/

Or, Scan the QR code!

Once you do, it will be intuitive. Enjoy, and thank you!

Sources

Bethell, Leslie. "Populism in Brazil." In *Brazil: Essays on History and Politics*, 175-194. University of London Press, 2018. http://www.jstor.org/stable/j.ctv51309x.10

Bethell, Leslie. "The Decline and Fall of Slavery in Brazil (1850-88)." In *Brazil: Essays on History and Politics*, 113-144. University of London Press, 2018. http://www.jstor.org/stable/j.ctv51309x.8

Bethell, Leslie. "The Long Road to Democracy in Brazil." In *Brazil: Essays on History and Politics*, 147-174. University of London Press, 2018. http://www.jstor.org/stable/j.ctv51309x.9

Bethell, Leslie, ed. *Colonial Brazil*. Cambridge University Press, 1987.

Burns, E. Bradford, Momsen, Richard P., Martins, Luciano, James, Preston E., and Schneider, Ronald Milton. "Brazil." *Encyclopedia Britannica*, August 28, 2024. https://www.britannica.com/place/Brazil

Fausto, B., and Fausto, S. *A Concise History of Brazil*. Cambridge University Press, 2014.

Martin, Percy Alvin. "Slavery and Abolition in Brazil." *The Hispanic American Historical Review* 13, no. 2 (1933): 151-196. https://doi.org/10.2307/2506690

Meade, T. A. *A Brief History of Brazil*. Infobase Publishing, 2010.

Newitt, M. *A History of Portuguese Overseas Expansion 1400-1668*. Routledge, 2004.

Putnam, Samuel. "Vargas Dictatorship in Brazil." *Science & Society* 5, no. 2 (1941): 97-116. http://www.jstor.org/stable/40399384

Teresa P. R. Caldeira, & Holston, J. "Democracy and Violence in Brazil." *Comparative Studies in Society and History* 41, no. 4 (1999): 691-729. http://www.jstor.org/stable/179426

Bierhorst, John
The Mythology of South America (1988)
Ardagh, Philip
South American Myths and Legends (1998)
Parker, Victoria
Traditional Tales from South America (2001)
Eells, Elsie Spicer
Fairy Tales from Brazil: How and Why Tales from Brazilian Folklore (2002)
Silva, Murilo Fidelis
Into the Wild: A Brief Journey into the Heart of Brazilian Folklore Legends (2023)
Cuscudo, Mario
Legends of the Amazon: Exploring Brazilian Mythology (2023)
Storm, Rachel and Carter, Geraldine
The Illustrated Guide to Latin American Mythology (1995)
Dorson, Mercedes and Wilmot, Jane
Tales from the Rain Forest: Myths and Legends from the Amazonian Indians of Brazil (1997)

Image Sources

[1] *https://commons.wikimedia.org/wiki/File:Henry_the_Navigator1.jpg*
[2] *https://commons.wikimedia.org/wiki/File:Capitanias.jpg*
[3] *https://commons.wikimedia.org/wiki/File:Jesus,_Benedito_Calixto_de_-_Domingos_Jorge_Velho_e_o_Loco-tenente_Ant%C3%B4nio_F._de_Abreu.jpg*
[4] *https://commons.wikimedia.org/wiki/File:Bandeira_da_Inconfid%C3%AAncia_1789_Os_Inconfidentes.jpg*
[5] *https://commons.wikimedia.org/wiki/File:Retrato_de_D._Jo%C3%A3o_VI,_Rei_de_Portugal.jpg*)
[6] . *https://commons.wikimedia.org/wiki/File:DpedroI-brasil-full.jpg*
[7] *https://en.wikipedia.org/wiki/File:Pedro_II_of_Brazil_-_Brady-Handy.jpg*
[8] *https://commons.wikimedia.org/wiki/File:Deodoro_da_Fonseca_(1889).jpg*
[9] *https://commons.wikimedia.org/wiki/File:Getulio_Vargas_(1930).jpg*
[10] *https://commons.wikimedia.org/wiki/File:Juscelino.jpg*

www.ingramcontent.com/pod-product-compliance
Lightning Source LLC
Chambersburg PA
CBHW070329010526
44107CB00004B/470